PRAISE FOR
MAKER TO MASTER

"*Maker To Master* will fast track creative business owners straight to success. Sue Monhait is a successful product entrepreneur and has worked with numerous other gifters, bakers, crafters and makers.

Sue's friendliness and enthusiasm shines through the pages and she is able to cover important business topics in an approachable and memorable way by weaving in her own stories and those of her clients.

I highly recommend this to any creative entrepreneur whether they are at the very beginning of their journey or are looking for fresh ideas for their current business."

Natalie Eckdahl, CEO, BizChix.com

"*Maker To Master* is a must-have book for every budding entrepreneur who wants to turn their hobby into a real business that makes real money. It's time to stop dreaming and start doing, or as I like to say, "Just Do It!" There are no more excuses because Sue shares what you need to know in order to achieve the success you've been yearning for."

Madalyn Sklar, Twitter Marketing Expert

"Sometimes it's hard to read books about business. We either feel the content and advice is not really applicable to us and we need to finangle the strategies to make them fit our business model, or we get overwhelmed with just how much we need to do. Or both.

This is NOT that book!

Sue Monhait does a MASTERFUL job of addressing the creative product makers market. Her book is not only easy to read and digest, but also helps the reader to understand she is not alone. That the frustrations and challenges she is facing have been faced – and overcome – by others, and that there is a clear step by step path to success! If you know your business has way more potential than your bank account is reflecting, then this book is for you.

Continue doing what you do best which is creating. Sue will show you how to get the business side of things running smooth and bring in the money to carry on."

Viveka von Rosen, CoFounder, Vengreso, #theLinkedInExpert

"Getting started on your entrepreneurial journey isn't easy and feeling stuck can become a common thing. To break through that, you need the right resources you can turn to for ideas, inspiration and motivation. Sue's book is filled with several stories that will do just that – so you can get back on the right path and make things happen!"

Kate Erickson, Creator, Engager, Implementer, Entrepreneurs On Fire

"If you are a creator and are stagnant or stuck and want to push forward and become the go to master at your craft, Sue's book, *Maker To Master*, helps you hone in on What's Not Working in your small biz and gives you the right strategies you need to fix them."

Sue B. Zimmerman, Founder, Susan B. Zimmerman Enterprise, #theinstagramexpert

MAKER

TO

MASTER

Find and Fix What's Not Working in Your Small Business

Dear Kria,
I'm so glad
we're now connected in
what you provide, a)
capturing memories is
so special and important
continue touching
all these hearts!
Best, Sue

SUE MONHAIT

Publishing Services by Happy Self Publishing
www.happyselfpublishing.com

Year: 2018

ISBN-13: 978-1718961661
ISBN-10: 1718961669

This book is dedicated to my husband, Michael
and my children David and Nichole.
You are my motivating light
and source of support
behind everything I do.

CONTENTS

———~———

INTRODUCTION

Jen had been looking forward to having coffee with Monica all week.

It was nothing extraordinary. They got together often, and it was always a special time; *Girl time*. Catching up, sharing stories about the kids, the next vacation, that sort of thing.

She remembers sitting with her cup of vanilla spiced latte and thinking about how lucky she was - great friends, a wonderful husband and two beautiful children.

She was truly blessed with her life ... until she wasn't.

How did this one coffee date change everything for her?

How did she go from being so grateful to now being anxious, stressed and resentful?

She shouldn't really blame Monica. It's not her fault. Except that it's all her fault in a way.

Jen tries to recollect how it all happened.

That morning they had both dropped off their children at school. Then they met at their regular high top wooden table near the window in the local coffee shop.

It was a favorite destination and the autumn day was sunny with a slight chill. A light breeze came through the open window that made the wind chimes tingle delicately in the background.

Monica noticed Jen's scarf and complimented her on it. It was a beautiful mixture of sage, mustard and tangerine - perfect for the season. And it had an interesting textured design with tassels on the ends.

"Oh, I made this," said Jen. "I've been knitting for years. It's relaxing and fun. I even make my own designs so I can try out new stitches."

"Really?" Monica reacted in surprise. "How is it we've been friends all this time and I didn't know that?"

"My sister's birthday is in a few weeks," Monica continued.

"Is there any chance you could make one for her? I'll pay you of course. It will be a fabulous gift. I just can't think of what else to get her. This would be really special!"

That was the start. It was perfect. Jen loved making her scarves and completely bought into the plan.

Of course, when the time came, she didn't accept money from Monica since she was a dear friend.

A few weeks later Monica told Jen how much her sister loved her gift. "Have you ever considered starting a knitting business? I bet a lot of people would be interested in your scarves," Monica stated emphatically.

That got Jen thinking. *Could I actually make money on the side while being home with the children? Why not?*

As her mind opened up, she liked the idea more and more.

So she started making scarves and selling to friends. It was energizing and exciting. People were eagerly buying them and things naturally developed from there.

She created a company called Jazzy Jen's. She built a website and everything. Jen was excited and proud to be a brand new entrepreneur.

Who would have ever thought I'd start a business of my very own? Jen remembered the satisfaction and joy in that thought.

Those days are now long gone. What started as a wonderful dream is now a disaster. Jen has spent a lot of money and for what?

Initially, her scarves were selling before she could even finish making them. Now sales are dribbling in - if you can even say that.

She has not reimbursed her parents for the money she borrowed to get started. It's been three years with little to show for it except a business card with Jazzy Jen's on it.

Jen's husband wants her to close down and she feels like a failure.

Perhaps the worst of this is that she really resents Monica. If she would never have put the idea of a business into her head, none of this would have happened.

Their friendship is now strained and she misses the camaraderie they once had.

It's not Monica's fault of course.

Jen has little time for coffee dates these days anyway. She's busy trying to turn this business around. If she has to shut down it will be humiliating and heartbreaking.

Where does she go from here?

Unfortunately, this scenario repeats itself every day. An innocent well-intended comment leads to an idea. The dream starts bright and opportunistic then fizzles away instead of growing to shine strong.

It's heartbreaking for all involved.

But it doesn't have to be this way.

This book is intended for Gifters-Bakers-Crafters-Makers of all sorts who have a dream to turn their hobby or craft into a business.

I may have caught you right where Jen is, having started a business and gotten stuck.

It's okay. Be forgiving with yourself. As a creator you have a lot of skill and knowledge. You know everything about your product. You have hard earned experience with equipment, tools and the various elements needed to produce your unique designs or delicious sweets.

I'm here to tell you the dream is achievable. You never needed to know the business side of things until now.

This book will guide you through the best practices of a thriving business.

Some may already be on your radar. But I bet there are a few that will be new and hold the key to getting you back on track and ensure your success.

There's not a minute to waste. Let's get started, shall we?

Idea Development

---〜---

IT'S ON MY MIND

It all begins with your dream.

Maybe you know you want to start your own business but haven't zoomed in on exactly what it is yet.

Or maybe you've thought it through in detail and just need to get started.

Perhaps you're on your way but have met up with obstacles you're struggling to overcome.

Before we go any further, it's important to review your vision. You are investing your heart into this dream, so let's confirm you're reaching for the right star.

By the end of this section you'll have the *right* full-color picture of your dream just waiting for you to make it come true.

It gets more and more exciting from there.

Chapter 1

IT'S A BRAND NEW WORLD

───────～───────

Congratulations! You have opened your mind to the dream of starting a business from your hobby or craft.

It's such an exciting time, because in your mind you can create anything—literally anything you want!

It's also the place every business starts. You're at the same point where Sheila was before she created Brownie Brittle. Where Katy was before she created The Leakey Collection. Where Pam was before she created Tuscany Tours.

This is a beautiful and dangerous place to be.

Let me explain.

It's easy at this stage to envision anything you want. The view from the outside, however, is always different than the view from the inside.

On the outside, we can dream of what we'd like the business to be. And dreams produce the feelings we want, too.

Here's where we can deceive ourselves. We dream about what we believe things will be like versus understanding the reality of our dream.

This is what happened to Sam. She loves everything associated with Bohemian style. A shop on Main Street was her vision. So, with a small loan, she started Bohemian Bliss and opened her doors.

She had such fun going to market and purchasing her first pieces of clothing, jewelry and gift items. What joy she took in picking out the perfect dusty rose paint for the walls that would be the backdrop for her beloved items. Stylish antique crystal chandeliers dropped from the ceiling offering extra ambiance. It was perfect!

And it truly was in the beginning.

Sam joined her local chamber and quickly became part of the community. Her customers enjoyed going to visit her to pick up gifts of all sorts. Her prices were quite reasonable and her items were unique and wonderfully quirky. She definitely had an eye for selecting what her customers wanted.

This sounds like a dream come true, doesn't it?

Bohemian Bliss closed its doors two years after it opened.

What happened?

In Sam's case, her dream did not align with reality. Sam was miserable in her store. She never considered that she would need to spend so much time in her shop every single day.

Sometimes nobody would come in for hours and she got bored. So, she'd hang a sign on the door and go to a yoga class, or grab lunch with a friend.

That didn't leave a good impression when someone came to buy a gift, only to find the shop closed. Most people don't have time to "Come back in an hour," as the sign directed. This only needed to happen a couple of times before word got around.

How do you prevent some version of this from happening to you?

As you consider turning your business dream into reality, take the time to live that reality in your mind. Unlike Sam, will you be able to handle the responsibility and commitment that a shop on Main Street requires?

Your specifics may be different. But before you get started and spend time and money, add a reality layer on top of your dream. Confirm to yourself that you are still as much in love with the idea as you think you are right now.

ADD A REALITY LAYER ON TOP OF YOUR DREAM.

Many are. And this is not meant to be a deterrent. If anything, it will push you to move forward.

It will create excitement and anticipation of what's to come. This is all very good!

Chapter 2

A RACING HEART

"**H**ow do I figure out what business I should start?"

I get asked this question often. Based on years of interviewing creators of all types, I've found that every idea starts in one of three ways:

A Childhood Joy. When we're young and societal norms haven't yet affected us, our true nature comes out. Think back to your childhood. What did you love to do when nobody controlled your time? Did you paint? Were you active with an outside activity? Did you like building with Legos?

Many bakers talk about the fond memories they have of spending time in the kitchen with a relative. Artists talk about getting their first coloring book or learning to knit with their grandmother. Creators of aromatherapy products speak of spending time in the garden among the many scents.

These moments in time are stored in our heart and reveal what really impacts and holds deep meaning for us.

What is it for you?

It's worth thinking about how this might be transformed into a business. These innate passions of your youth might be something that will give you joy and fulfillment for a lifetime.

A Racing Heart. Our body gives us signals that we don't even realize. Tuning in and recognizing these signals can pay off big time!

Here I have to tell of my own experience:

Shortly after Michael and I married, we took a trip to France. Our tour brought us from Paris to Provence to Marseille. I fell in love with the country. I reveled in the never-ending fields of sunflowers and lavender. There were quaint villages with small nooks and crannies to discover. I couldn't get enough of the bold bright colors and flavorful delicacies of all sorts—and the wine!

One day we were on our tour bus winding through one of these small towns. The road was so narrow the homes on each side could be touched by stretching an arm out the window. That allowed me to curiously peek inside the homes through the lace curtains. I admit it!

I so enjoyed looking at the decor. What caught my eye most were the linens. The bold royal blue, brilliant yellow and bright passionate red. I couldn't get enough.

Our bus turned a bend and there on the corner was an outdoor market with all these beautiful Provencal linens displayed.

My heart was racing. I was praying with all my might that we would stop so I could immerse myself amongst all that color. Lucky for me we did!

Yes, I bought more than my fair share of linens - which I have to this day.

As I reflect back, the physical effect of this experience was amazing. My body was telling me about what I love. It wasn't, "Oh that's so pretty." It was much more than that.

Others I've talked to have had similar physical reactions to different events. For you it might be how you feel when your hands interact with clay. Or the instant joy you experience as you search for the right fabrics for your next quilt.

A physical sign can also be a heartfelt reaction. This happened to both Pam and Stacey when they were traveling abroad.

Pam fell in love with Tuscany on her very first trip. The food and wine, the art and landscapes, and the people. It impacted her so deeply that she and her husband, Sam moved from America and they raised their family in a small medieval village near Siena.

She also started Tuscany Tours, so she could share her love of the country with others.

What fun Pam now has as she sees her country anew through the eyes of her tourists.

For Stacey it was a family trip to Peru. With a natural flair for art and design, she loved the patterns and native styles surrounding her on the streets and in the shops. But she also noticed the poverty and the struggles these beautiful Peruvian women endured.

When Stacey returned home, she couldn't shake the feeling that something needed to be done to help these women.

That led her to founding Shopping for a Change, a non-profit that empowers impoverished women across the globe.

Being conscious of the clues your body sends you is nature's way of saying, "Do more of that."

How wonderful if you can incorporate this into your new business!

A Random Moment. This is often how the idea for a new product originates. Someone is just going through their day and BAM—a problem arises and the need for a solution exposes itself.

This is exactly what happened to Tom. Upon retirement, Tom was assigned the household task of keeping the bird feeder full.

This will be easy, he thought. Until the squirrels started wreaking havoc. No sooner would he fill the feeder when the squirrels would come along and empty it out.

This interruption to Tom's newfound free time simply would not do. Particularly on a Sunday afternoon during football season. After a little thought and ingenuity, Squirrel Away Bird Cafe was born.

Sometimes it's not a solution to a problem but more an instantaneous idea. That's how Amy's company, Marshmallow MBA came about. She was having a holiday drink with her friend, Keith.

They were enjoying a marshmallow treat she whipped up with her grandmother's original recipe. Keith was the one who suggested she turn this into a business.

The idea took a while to settle in. Amy challenged whether there would actually be a market for her marshmallows. But once that was proven, there was no stopping her.

Ideas for businesses are around us every single day. If you are looking for that perfect idea, consider any or all of these three triggers and keep a watchful eye. The right idea will appear for you—maybe even tomorrow!

Chapter 3

ANOTHER SERVING?

———————⁓———————

Let's talk about the concept of success. Our culture steers us in the direction that success means more money, growth or fame. Supposedly, to be successful, you must continually do more and more of whatever it is you do.

The thinking goes that when you get more you will also be happier, fulfilled and free.

Whoa ... let's back it up.

This is a nice idea but far from the truth.

We see lots of demonstrations that this isn't so. From actors who are overdosing to top CEOs who have heart attacks; there are signs all around that the concept that "more is better" is a fallacy.

I'm very lucky to have quite a few awesome friends. I want to introduce you to several of them.

Joanne has been a professional career woman from the beginning. She has worked for her prestigious company for over 25 years. She is a star in her department and eats, lives and breathes her job.

She makes a great living and has stock in her company too. That will pay off handsomely when she retires in a few years. Yes, she has to deal with the politics of a corporate job, but as long as she is focused on her performance, she's good!

To say Marie is a woman of many interests and passions is putting it mildly. She plays tennis, runs, is involved in book groups and charitable activities and oh yes—works part time too. There have been years when she has worked a couple of part time jobs.

To her, being able to jump from event to event throughout her day fuels and satisfies her. She continually mixes things up based on her interests and what excites her and gives her life purpose at that time.

Naomi is a "traditional" stay-at-home mom to three school-age children. Do you have as much respect and admiration for this lifestyle and job as I do?

Naomi is all about making the childhood experience exceptional through direct contact and interaction. Her days are filled with planning, transportation, volunteer school activities and more.

Each of these women is living a successful life by their own standards. But they move through completely different days. Who is to say that one woman is more successful than another?

None of us. But it's where we sometimes get tangled up in self-doubt—because we compare ourselves to others.

Each of us has our own life to live. And in the end, each of us should determine what it means to be successful for ourselves. Without outside influences, without comparison to others, without judgment.

In business, success can mean different things too. For some it's a little extra spending money. Or it's being able to pay for spring break or summer camp every year. For others it may mean keeping a business small while the children are young and at home. Or it may be building a multi-million-dollar company.

When you start to monetize your activities, the notion of "more" tends to kick in.

You may think:

"I need to move out of my home-based business and have a retail shop."

OR

"My revenue needs to increase year after year."

OR

"I should broaden my line and add production staff."

Here's a shocker. Growing bigger could grow you right out of your passion.

GROWING BIGGER COULD GROW YOU RIGHT OUT OF YOUR PASSION.

It's possible that growing bigger might cause your daily activities to change. They could go from creating a product to supervising a team. Or from interacting with customers to negotiating leases and building websites. These may be things that you don't enjoy, and all of a sudden, you've created a devil in disguise.

What happened to the energy and excitement that had you jumping out of bed to greet each day?

You grew yourself right out of what you love to do!

This is why it's important to be crystal clear on what you want. Write it on a piece of paper, put it in the memos app in your phone, or put a Post-it note on your bulletin board.

It sounds so basic and simple but it produces powerful results.

A business and a life that energizes and excites you. That's success.

Chapter 4

THEY'RE NOT YOUR FRIENDS

———— ∿ ————

Friends play a very special role in our life. I'm sure you're a lot like me in this regard. I cherish my friends and consider them a true blessing. I value our time together and the special secrets and memories we've created and shared.

We also support each other's endeavors even when they are different from our own. I see these as signs of true friendship.

It's natural then to talk about your business dream with a friend. They can be a sounding board and provide emotional support.

But they cannot, I repeat *cannot* be the single source of affirmation that you are onto a good idea.

It's only natural that their comments will be tainted. They don't want to hurt your feelings or offend you. Feedback will be skewed in your favor even if unintentionally.

Amy recognized this to be true. She devised a unique way to get honest opinions of her new product from her friends. And she could do it while she was in the same room and could witness their reactions. It was brilliant!

Amy owns a company called Kuhfs. This is a fashion accessory that transforms your jeans or boots into different styles. It's a way to update your existing wardrobe and vary the look based on any occasion.

In development mode, Amy would wear her Kuhfs while she was out with friends. When asked about them, she didn't reveal that it was her product. In this way she was able to get true reactions and feedback on the concept.

Over time, Amy revealed the secret and used some of these friends to further test her designs and give recommendations as she perfected the sizing and style.

Sharing your business idea with friends and getting their opinion is important. The input you get is invaluable. Just remember to keep it in perspective and consider it as one part of the overall opinion poll.

There is definitely another very special role for your friends. They are the ones you invite to celebration parties when you reach milestones along the way!

Chapter 5

BANISH THE LIAR

———⁓———

W e're brought up to be honest. To always tell the truth. Say it like it is in a sympathetic and caring way. So why don't we follow this direction when talking to ourselves?

We are liars or even bullies with our self-talk when we should be our most loyal advocates.

How often do you say things like:

"That person is so much smarter than me," or

"I could never do what she's doing," or

"I'm pretending to be something I'm not."

Have you ever made the mistake of calling someone by the wrong name? It's embarrassing and then you berate yourself long into the future.

The same plays out for your business overall. You say to yourself,

"You're so stupid. How could you say that?" or

"Why in the world did you think you could be successful at that?" or

"I told you this would end badly. It's for anyone else but not you."

I'm right, aren't I? You are lying to yourself.

This is such common thinking there are even terms for the behavior. We each have an *inner critic* and suffer from *imposter syndrome.*

The key is to not let it get in your way. You need to shut down this thinking. Stand up to your inner critic and say, "I'll have no more of this!"

How do you overcome the defeatist thinking that prevents you from achieving all that you can be?

It begins with understanding that everyone experiences self-doubt talk from time to time. Recognizing this can bring peace and acceptance.

Even well-known speakers and vocal artists tell us that they still get nervous before going on stage. Why should they? They've performed and proven themselves over and over again.

It's because it is human nature. We can't avoid it.

What needs to happen is a mindset makeover. Reposition your thinking to accept the fact that there will be times when you are uncomfortable. Embrace this feeling knowing that you are stretching yourself and that you are growing with your experiences.

By taking action you are moving your plan forward. It is what others who you aspire to be like have done. They move past the uncomfortable.

They aren't able to shut it *off*. They just shut it *down*.

Finally, instead of looking at and judging yourself, refocus on impacting those around you. What help are you providing through a volunteer event? What are you teaching people when you speak to a group? How does your product enrich the lives of those who buy it?

It's almost a miracle how, when you focus and serve others, your inner critic is forgotten. There is no time to think about yourself. You need to focus on them.

WHEN YOU FOCUS AND SERVE OTHERS, YOUR INNER CRITIC IS FORGOTTEN.

Stand up to the liar in you. Be impolite and talk back with the truth. That you are deserving. That you do have the skills and passion to be and do what you are striving for.

You have a lot to share with the world and how dare that lying inner critic stand in your way!

Chapter 6

WHY IS THIS A SECRET!?

—————～—————

Some people don't believe it but I'm totally in. I've seen it time and time again.

The Law of Attraction. Putting thoughts out into the universe and having them come back with an answer or a solution. It's a little freaky.

Throughout history, people have sensed that there is something more powerful than what we can see. There is a natural force out there that, when prompted by our thoughts, can actually make things happen.

THERE IS A NATURAL FORCE OUT THERE THAT, WHEN PROMPTED BY OUR THOUGHTS, CAN ACTUALLY MAKE THINGS HAPPEN.

Ten years ago, I had a home-based gift basket business called Basket Thyme. My vision of making money while staying home with the children didn't quite work out. The business continued to grow and grow. It got to the point where I could no longer have employees coming into my basement to fill orders. It was time to move out.

I was coming to this realization when I found myself in line at the post office talking with a woman in front of me. Our conversation turned to business and I mentioned my dilemma.

She passed on information about a space right near her office that had become available. As I drove by to check out the location, I almost slammed on the breaks in awe.

The open space was a building I had driven by the week prior. At that time a thought went through my mind, *If ever I need to expand, this is the kind of place I'd like to find.*

Seriously!?!

I signed the deal within a week.

Okay. We can mark this off to coincidence. I'll go with you there. But listen to what happened next.

Over the next five years, I found another business opportunity and passion. My gift basket business was steadily growing, but my mind and heart went elsewhere. I saw a worldwide market and a huge opening in this new direction. So, I decided I would wind down Basket Thyme and ramp up the new business over a two-year period.

One summer day my husband and I were walking in downtown Highland Park. Our community is a quaint village right on the water about 20 miles north of Chicago. We are lucky to have a beautiful downtown that is conducive to afternoon strolling, shopping and dining al fresco. You get the picture.

That afternoon I made the comment that I would love to move into an office in this historic area.

For the new business I wouldn't need all the space I currently had, and the work lifestyle was important to me. I envisioned being able to walk to work. The idea of grabbing coffee or lunch with a friend was appealing too. Or taking mid-day walks next to Lake Michigan.

Wouldn't you know ... the next week I had a meeting at our Chamber of Commerce and the space next to them had just opened up.

The space was a problem for most potential occupants because of its layout. It had two windowless, unusually shaped rooms and two beautiful windowed offices. For most it was terrible. For me it was perfect!

Yep. You guessed it. With tape measure in hand, I confirmed the space would fit my needs. Today, The Ribbon Print Company calls this location home.

I am a firm believer that our mind and thoughts are far more powerful than we understand.

So be brave and dream big. Put words to your ideas and see what can appear. It's as if you've ordered it up from a menu.

Now you have a detailed vision of the business you want to create. You have confirmed that it fits into your life and aligns with your personality. You are ready to start taking concrete action.

Many people jump right in at this point with the most obvious and fun activities; the company name and logo.

But hold tight. If you want this new business of yours to thrive, there are other things you need to put in place first.

We cover these next.

Planning

---~---

READY, SET, GO!

Let's compare creating your business to planting a flower.

In the first chapter, you were deciding what flower you wanted to plant. You narrowed it down and made your choice. Now you know when you plant your seed what type of flower should appear.

Next you need to select the right area for your flower. It needs the appropriate amount of sunlight and soil of good quality.

If you plant a seed in gravel and shade, it should be no surprise when it doesn't grow.

It's the same with your business. For the flower to bloom vibrant and strong, there are things you need to do beneath the surface to ensure its growth.

Chapter 7

MOVE IT!

———————$\sim$———————

You have them. I do too. We all have friends who say, "I'm going to write that book," or, "I want to open my own shop."

But they never do.

Years go by. They continue talking.

Nothing happens.

Maybe it's just talk. But if they've said it over and over, it's more likely they've fallen into one of the most paralyzing traps of all—their own mind.

It's scary to put yourself out there and go for your dream.

Committing through words is a great first step but until action is taken there is nothing to show for all the talk.

There are two reasons people don't take action: they are either afraid of failing or they don't know how to take the first step.

Let's talk about both of these.

If you haven't been in the entrepreneurial world for long, you're going to have to trust me on this.

Even the most successful among us, not only has the fear of failure, but has failed. And I'd wager to bet they have failed many times.

We look in on other people's businesses and think that what they have today was created on the first try. Social media reinforces this belief since all the images and posts present the best of what a company has to offer.

If you dive into the backstory of every company, you'll find struggles and challenges. The business owner felt defeated and discouraged along the way.

Knowing this is helpful. You can remind yourself that it's part of the game. You can punch self-doubt in the face and not allow it to prevent you from taking action.

But then what action is it that you should take?

If knowledge is what is preventing you from moving forward, then shame on you. Sorry for the tough love here. But you have all the resources you need at literally the touch of a finger.

Remember that six-letter friend, Google? Ask away and you'll be surprised with all that will appear on your computer screen.

I see this demonstrated in my podcast interviews over and over again. It's the little steps that build on each other that allows someone to accomplish big things.

Push yourself to keep going. Take that next little step and then another and another. This is a process.

Chapter 8

NICE TO MEET YOU

N aming your business is a big deal. You have to love it. You are going to think it, say it and dream about it. A lot!

Here are some guidelines to consider as you test out different name ideas.

Consider your long-term business intent. It seems crazy to think about how you'll exit your business right as you're starting. But when it comes to a name, this is important. If you plan to sell down the road, a business named after you is less attractive to a buyer.

Maureen's Sweet Shoppe is run by a passionate, gentle and affectionate woman of the same name. The business loses its magnetism if it's sold and is run by the quirky tattoo-loving Jizel. In this instance, Maureen is the brand and of significant value to the company. Without her there is a disconnect.

A company with a more generic name is in a stronger position when it comes to transition of ownership.

What would Martha Stewart's company be without her? What is the value of Rachel Ray's enterprise without Rachel's presence overlaying all that the company does?

You may see these big brands as not applicable to your situation, but it is the same. Maybe even more so because being a local small business owner, people will know you personally. Removing yourself from your business changes everything.

Consider the location of your business. The same goes for a company named after a physical location such as a street or town name.

Santa Barbara Gift Baskets in California would not be the same if Anne picked up and moved her business to Colorado.

If you know with 100% certainty that your business will always be located right in your community, then a location name can add connectivity.

In Anne's case, she promotes products made from artisans right in her area. This reinforces and gives depth to the name. Residents of Santa Barbara and the surrounding area naturally feel connected.

If you don't think you'll sell your business or move it to another town, then feel free to incorporate these identifying themes into your company name.

Apart from these two cautions, go wild with creativity and find a fun, unique and memorable name.

It may include your product by name, like Lucas Chocolates. Or it may be a play on your product like The Mad Soyentist or Twice Baked Pottery.

But don't limit yourself to that either.

How do you come up with a great name?

To help you along, I've created a Name Generation Workbook. It's an exercise that helps identify creative names that resonate with you based on things you love. Gather several friends to help and you'll be surprised by the options you'll have.

You can find the free Name Generator Workbook at GiftBizUnwrapped.com/namegenerator.

After you narrow down and select your name, the next step is to make sure that it's available. You want to confirm it's not trademarked and used by someone else. You can do this easily online.

Once your chosen name has passed this first test, there is another important step. Make sure the domain name (in the .com extension) and all social media sites you plan to use are also available.

When naming your business, you want to give it the attention it needs. But don't dwell on this step for too long and have it hinder your progress. There comes a time when you have to make a choice and move on.

Chapter 9

DIVIDE AND CONQUER

———⁓———

I'm going directly to the bottom line here (which is so appropriate since we're now talking about money).

You must create a separate bank account for your business.

Why?

The very future of your life and your business depends on it.

Just ask Jeanne. She sold her maple-glazed cinnamon caramel apples first as single sales to friends. As her sales grew she ventured out to local craft shows. Now she wholesales to regional gourmet shops.

But along the way her business almost melted away.

Jeanne took short cuts as she started her business. Since she was so small, she didn't consider keeping her money separate. Opening a dedicated account for the company wasn't even on her radar.

She did what many new business owners do. She used her personal account to purchase product and equipment. She charged the printing of business cards and flyers to her visa card, along with her regular groceries and other personal expenses.

Everything came out of one account.

That worked for a while. Months went by and more and more caramel apples were being made and sold. Jeanne was thrilled. She was making money and running a successful business.

So she thought.

About six months into her venture, she realized her mistake. The end of the month approached. In the mail came her bank statement, credit card statements and all the other bills. She paid them as usual and carried on with her day.

But 48 hours later, everything fell apart. She totally forgot about her mortgage and her daughter's new dance team uniform. These were due immediately and she had nothing left in her account!

Jeanne's error came when she decided to upgrade her equipment and commit to a commercial kitchen lease. At that time, she looked at how much money she had in her bank account and felt confident that she could cover it all.

In actuality she had only nine dollars and 27 cents to her name.

Not paying the mortgage would affect Jeanne's credit rating and not being able to get her daughter's pink sequin dance uniform ... unthinkable!

In the end, Jeanne borrowed from her family to make ends meet. And she learned a valuable lesson.

Combining business and personal finances is dangerous.

Now she has two separate accounts. She understands what her financial situation is for both at any given time.

Doing this is very simple. When you first start your business, dedicate a certain amount of money as a "startup" loan to yourself. Let's say it's $500. Open a bank account with a debit card. Your first balance is that $500.

As your business brings in money, you can repay yourself for the initial loan. Then watch your business grow in and of its own right.

Chapter 10

THESE BOOTS ARE MADE FOR WALKING

Investopedia defines bootstrapping as follows, "An individual is said to be bootstrapping when he or she attempts to found and build a company from personal finances or from the operating revenues of the new company."

Bootstrapping is funding your business without taking out bank loans. This requires an initial investment that should be set up in a separate bank account as we reviewed in the prior section "Divide and Conquer."

With that first influx of money, you will need to prioritize what is most important to invest in first.

For our community of Gifts-Bakers-Crafters-Makers, you obviously have to buy the elements you need to make your product. It's the yarn or beads if you make fashion accessories. It's the flour, sugar and milk if you make cupcakes.

Other priorities are initial startup costs such as registering your business and opening a bank account.

As your business grows and you start to make money, you can develop the business further. You'll want to put up a website, secure a dedicated email address, etc.

But in the early stages there are always low cost or no cost options.

Start with free social media platforms to grow your audience and promote your products. Use a free google email account and transition to a business account later. By this I mean a google account yourbizname@gmail.com (free account) versus yourname@yourbusinessname.com (paid business account).

When you bootstrap, you grow your business slower. But for many it is the responsible way to go. If your family counts on your income to cover the monthly bills, you do not need the added pressure of one more payment and incurring interest on a loan.

The best thing about bootstrapping is you emotionally realize success earlier. When you spend only what you know you can afford, the bank balance you see on your statement is in the black. As the balance goes up and up you know you're making true money. Even if it's a small increase each month, it's real and it's yours!

THE BEST THING ABOUT BOOTSTRAPPING IS YOU EMOTIONALLY REALIZE SUCCESS EARLIER.

I bootstrapped both my multi six-figure businesses and would do it again. There is something to be said for being able to sleep well at night. And being able to focus on how to grow your business; not stressing about how you're going to pay an overdue bill.

Chapter 11

THAT'S ALL THERE IS?

———— ∽ ————

The riches are in the niches. It's a popular phrase these days and oh so true.

In the marketing days gone by, we called it a core product. Same thing.

The best way I can demonstrate this concept is through a story … about you.

The phone rings and it's your doctor's office.

"The results of the skin sample we tested are in," Dr. Harrison begins. "It is melanoma on your upper right arm. We must address this immediately."

You knew all those years in the sun were putting you at risk. But you took your chances anyway.

Of course, this is bad news but there is a silver lining. It has been caught early and with minor surgery and regular checkups, it is manageable and not life threatening.

But action needs to be taken. What do you do now?

Dr. Harrison says that you can come into her office and she can take care of it for you. Or you can go to a specialist who can do the same procedure.

Melanoma ... this can be serious.

My guess is you would choose to go to someone who focuses specifically on this disease versus going to a general practitioner.

Your fictional story is now over. I'm so glad you're okay.

Let's now apply this example to your business.

By narrowing in and focusing on a specific product or service, you become a specialist in that category.

Your specialty then provides direction for all you do moving forward. It defines your target customer, your messaging, and the platforms you select to get in front of the right people. It's like gold!

For a great example, we can look to Kara of Kara's Vineyard Wedding.

Are you ready for this?

Her business started around wine corks used as place cards for weddings. No, I'm not joking. She has built an entire business around this initial core product.

As her business developed, she expanded into related products such as Christmas ornaments and wine charms. She also hosts a podcast focused on wedding planning.

You will notice they are all spinoffs of the original idea, only brought to life *because of* the initial momentum she gained thanks to niching way down with her first idea.

The larger and more disjointed your product offering is at the start, the more you become "vanilla" to the market.

This makes it all too easy for people to go someplace else to find an expert who can help solve their specific pain point.

The more niched down you are, the more attractive and unique you become.

That attracts sales.

Chapter 12

HI! I KNOW YOU!

———— ∾ ————

O nce you've decided on your product and its specific niche, it's time to define who your customer is. This is referred to as an avatar.

No, it's not everyone who breathes and could potentially use your product. It is that select group of people for whom the product is made. It's those who are naturally attracted to your business because of what you stand for and what your product is.

This can be a hard concept to wrap your head around. It's similar to the challenge of narrowing down your product as we discussed in the last section.

It's extremely important and has tremendous value as you move forward.

When you are able to define your avatar, you can communicate on a deeper level. Your prospects will feel like you are talking directly to them. They will feel you "get" them.

Francesca is a jewelry designer. She defines her market as young teenage or college girls who want to be seen as trendsetters in their social group. Her designs are always slightly pushing the limits. She pays particular attention to color and material to ensure her styles are current.

By defining her customer as she has, the wording in her promotions is not:

"Come see our large assortment of accessories. You're sure to find something you love that will look great on you."

This is way too general and resonates with ... nobody.

Check this out:

"Prom is next weekend. You've got your dress but how do you make yourself stand out? On display now is a new collection of ear and nose rings in colors hot off the runway. Come pick out the one that is calling your name and be the envy of all your friends."

Or:

"It's spring break and you're headed to the beach. We're thinking you need a new belly button ring to go with your tan. But beware! It's sure to spark interest from that guy you have eyes for."

See the difference? By defining your avatar, you can use specific wording and imagery that make your customer certain you are the one and only place to buy.

It's because they recognize that you understand them inside and out.

These examples are in line with Francesca's customer and not in line with a middle-aged career woman. That's intentional and it results in sales.

There is more to this too. When you define your customer in detail, it will help direct where you should advertise to capture more of the same audience. From printed brochures to Facebook ads, you can target and invest in the right platforms where your ideal customer resides.

If you've not done this yet, find time to do so now. Create your own ideal avatar. Even name her and describe how she looks. Decide on her age, income and education level. But don't stop there.

Think about what movies she likes to watch, what magazines she reads and what she does in her spare time. The more detailed you can get, the more powerful your avatar will be.

Then, when you are putting together social media posts or print ads, speak to this person directly. Not every customer of yours, just this one person. You will see the difference in results. I guarantee it!

Chapter 13

GRAB YOUR PEN AND PAPER

———⟨∾⟩———

We get back to what seems like a completely irrational idea; selling your business when you are just opening up.

Right now, you are thinking about the excitement and the many rewards that await you by owning and working in your business.

Selling is the last thing on your mind.

You're right! You should love what you are starting. You should be filled with anticipation. You're envisioning many days of dedicated work within the framework of your developing business.

Wouldn't it be something, however, to make money not only while you are active in your business but also after you've decided to move on to something else in life?

MAKE MONEY NOT ONLY WHILE YOU ARE ACTIVE IN YOUR BUSINESS BUT ALSO AFTER YOU'VE DECIDED TO MOVE ON TO SOMETHING ELSE IN LIFE.

If this appeals to you, the actions you take now will make everything so much easier later.

It starts with the name of your company. We've already covered this in the "Nice to Meet You" section. If you missed it make sure to go back and review.

As demonstrated in Michael Gerber's book *E-Myth Revisited*, you also want to set up systems within your business right from the start. These are ways of running your business that can be documented in a step by step fashion.

When you have systems, they can be replicated by someone other than you. This is a best practice for any business but mandatory if you want to sell your company for any significant amount of money in the future.

Creating systems has two benefits.

While you run your company, it allows you to grow your business easier and faster. If you are adding employees, training is smooth because there is a process to follow. If you add a second shop, you will be up and running quicker because there is already an established way of doing things.

Documented systems and processes are even more important when it comes time to sell. The value of a business includes not only sales, secret recipes and patents. It also includes the processes used to run the company.

The way you order products, the onboarding of a new employee, how you handle a customer through a sale are all things that can be made into a process.

Because *you* have created the way to do things, these processes are unique to your business and they are worth money—if they are documented.

Someone who is interested in buying your business will be attracted to the fact that there can be a smooth transition through a handoff.

So how do you do this documentation? It's easy. As you create new systems, capture the steps that are part of the process from beginning to end.

Think of it as a recipe. First you have the ingredients and then you have the steps to make a dish. That is a process.

If your business is up and running, you'll find many systems exist already. Start by documenting those.

For a new business, documenting as you go will put you in great shape for the future.

Let's complete the flower analogy I started at the beginning of this section. You have now planted your flower seed in a stable environment. Your field of flowers are ready to grow and bloom.

In a perfect world you'd be set to flourish now and into the future.

But there are some nasty weeds coming up amongst your sprouting flowers.

These weeds are your competitors and we need to deal with them next.

Competition

---~---

PEEK A BOO!

Competition. We don't get a choice. Competitors. They exist.

When it comes to your competitors, you *get to* choose the way you want to react. There are two options.

You can play small by cowering and succumbing to their real or perceived power.

Or you can stare them down and strategize how you will win.

I'll show you next where you have the power and how you can make your competition disappear.

Chapter 14

FINDING THE HIDDEN TREASURE

———— ~ ————

"Being different is better than being better." When you truly understand this quote by Sally Hogshead, it leads to magic.

Identifying a unique attribute for your business or product brings strength to your brand and helps attract your ideal audience.

When you add unique qualities to your business, people will follow and buy from you because they resonate with what makes you different. Your customers will be supportive and, more importantly, loyal.

WHEN YOU ADD UNIQUE QUALITIES TO YOUR BUSINESS, PEOPLE WILL FOLLOW AND BUY FROM YOU BECAUSE THEY RESONATE WITH WHAT MAKES YOU DIFFERENT.

In this world of price cutting and nondescript brands, standing out is refreshing and will grab attention.

I call this your Unique Special Power.

USP is normally an acronym for a unique selling proposition. I find that old school and focuses too much on the selling of your product. In other words, pushing your product outwards for an audience to buy.

A Unique Special Power goes the opposite direction. It attracts people to your product because they connect with your uniqueness.

I'll demonstrate with one of my favorite examples. Let me introduce you to Katy Leakey of The Leakey Collection.

Are you familiar with Zulugrass necklaces? This jewelry is sourced and made by the Masaii women in the Riff Valley of East Africa.

Katy is onto something here. She actually has **two** Unique Special Powers.

Zulugrass is not found anywhere else in the world, so beads made from this local grass cannot be replicated. It makes her product truly one-of-a-kind.

She tells of how a company in China tried to knock off her necklaces. The problem was they didn't have Zulugrass. They only had plastic beads. So, it didn't work.

It's the texture of the beads and how they take color that makes Katy's necklaces so beautiful.

The story of the Masaii women making the necklaces is the second Unique Special Power. These women employ their men to work for them. Does that make you smile as much as it does me?

These women now all have businesses, in a third world country no less, and are standing on their own two feet. They are embracing change and their future.

There are many ways you can create a USP for your business. It could be in your product as in Katy's case. It could be the location of your shop if it's in a historic district or an old icehouse from the late 1800's. It could be in the unique patterns that are recognizable in only your brand such as Vera Bradley or Lily Pulitzer. Or perhaps in a shape that becomes symbolic to your product like Brighton's hearts.

There are an unlimited number of ways you can make your company different and stand out. Story, product, shape, color, location, scent, the options are limitless. It's well worth figuring out the Unique Special Power that is you.

Chapter 15

THAT'S A BIG GUY!

———— ∼ ————

Over the last few decades we've seen a wave of big brands wash over America.

Walmart expanded and uprooted many small-town shops. Today you can go into Target, a thousand miles from home, and find the same things you can buy back in your local Target store.

These chains appear from the outside to have the edge. They have purchasing power for sure. It's assumed that their systems, from strategy and marketing to inventory and sales, are done in the most sophisticated and effective ways.

How can you as a small business ever go up against that?

Good news! There are many ways a smaller business has the edge.

By nature, a large company has numerous reporting levels and rules. With this comes their weakness.

We've all heard about (or even experienced) corporate politics. There's accountability, paperwork and lots of covering your a**.

Subordinates want to look good in front of their supervisors. Departments compete against each other. They all think their division is the most valuable to the business ... and egos reign supreme.

Yes, I'm generalizing here. But when layoffs are announced, and pink slips are passed out, even the best of corporations find this behavior increase.

No wonder so many people want to escape this day-to-day work existence!

You, as the founder of your business, steer your own ship. You are released from the waters of corporate muck and can sail free.

You have the advantages of speed and flexibility on your side.

I'm sure you know that the ability to attract and get close to your customer results in higher sales.

Over the last few years, corporations have started to understand the role of social media and its ability to connect with customers. But it is the small businesses that have acted first and in a big way.

It will take a while for most large brands to figure out how use social media effectively. Many still have mental restraints that have to be worked through.

"What if one of our employees posts something embarrassing?"

"What if our product is represented in a bad light?"

"The pictures won't be of the quality we're known for. "

Transparency for a corporation is threatening. The idea of losing control is, for many, unimaginable.

Social media is just one area illustrating the time it takes to institute change in large enterprises. They are slow-moving cruise ships and you are a high-speed luxury yacht.

Being nimble enough to test things quickly and pivot or go all in is something that a large business can't do.

But you can. It's a huge advantage.

Chapter 16

BE RUDE. IGNORE THEM!

———————— ∽ ————————

Competition. Wouldn't the world be so much better if it went away? Guess what? In a way it can!

When you are starting out, you need to check out the competition. You want to understand how many competitors you have. You want to know what they offer, what their price points are and how they work with their customers.

This gives insight into where you can slip into the market to fill a void and attract a different group of customers.

But after that, your focus should shift completely off your competition.

Once you have an established solid base of customers, all eyes should be on them.

Understanding what they love about your product and why they support you and then doing more of the same will endear them to you.

Focusing on how you can make your product or service increasingly better for your customer is why they will continue to stay by your side.

In this way, you will create a divide between you and your competition. You aren't copying them and presenting more of the same to your market. You are doubling down on enhancing your own business.

I'll give you a caution though. Your less-educated competitors will begin copying you. It's so frustrating. Can't they think for themselves?

I've had this happen to me many times at The Ribbon Print Company. We created a new product because it helped our customers decrease their production time. Copied.

We developed our own brand of ribbon made specifically for use with our printers. What happened? A competitor now offers (on a limited scale) an imitation of ours. They even named it something similar. Seriously? Can't they think up their own innovations?

It's infuriating, and I have to remind myself it's also a form of flattery.

Off my rant now but it makes a point.

You can never go wrong when you stay close to your customer. Continually provide them with more and more of what they want. They will see that you listen and care about their needs.

Honestly, it's much more fun hanging out with them than spying on someone else anyway!

The advantages you have as a small business are powerful when recognized and used. That and having complete focus on your customers will guide you in all areas of your business.

This includes product selection, pricing and inventory control.

It is the place where we, as Gifts-Bakers-Crafters-Makers, unintentionally slide off track.

Make sure to pay close attention as we move forward.

Product Management

I'M MOVING IN

Admit it. I know you do it. You give away or underprice your products ... a lot.

We are notorious for not appreciating our talents to their full financial extent. Because creativity comes so naturally to us, we think our skills are not worth money.

That leads us to underprice or not include production time at all when we determine our product's price. When the entire business is priced in this way, it will lead to financial failure.

We're talking money on several levels next. I'm going to show you how to make sure you aren't unconsciously buying or pricing yourself right out of your dream.

Chapter 17

DON'T TOUCH!

———～———

It's natural as a new business owner to want to sell products that you like best.

You love making turquoise jewelry or you prefer lemon cake over carrot cake. Naturally these would be the items you think of first to include in your store or on your website.

But you have to be careful here. Your customer is not you. You think you know what they will purchase. But you can't be certain until you get those first sales and learn about your customers' preferences.

I remember back when I had my gift basket business. I loved my beautiful breakfast basket design and knew it would be a top seller. It had gourmet coffee, blueberry pancake mix, lemon biscotti and maple syrup in a glass leaf jar ... all nestled into a big rattan basket shaped like a coffee cup. Adorable!

But it didn't sell.

It took me two years and continually replacing expired product before I finally "got it." My customers were not interested in the coffee basket design I loved so much.

Stubbornly keeping that design was a waste of money and inventory space. I should have recognized it much earlier.

I've seen this repeated by others many times when they go to market to find new items for their stores. It's easy to get caught up in the moment by something new that you love.

When this happens, take a step back and think about your customer. Is a version of this product already a top seller for you? Have people come in asking for the product so you know there is demand?

As time goes on you'll learn more and more about your customers' likes and dislikes. There will be times that you misjudge and have to mark down product just to clear it out.

As you learn you'll get wiser and become a pro at stocking items that move quickly.

It becomes a skill that you acquire over time.

Chapter 18

WHO ARE YOU?

———⌇———

"**H**ow much is it?" I'm guessing if we took a poll, this would be the most frequently asked shopping question worldwide. It's a phrase translated in every tour book. I've learned it in more than a few languages throughout my travels.

What's the first thing you think of when you're asked this question?

My guess is you try to figure out if you can give a price *low* enough to be acceptable. Right?

Why is this? Why do we automatically think that if we don't drop our price, we'll lose the sale? This price-cut mentality has to stop.

WHY DO WE AUTOMATICALLY THINK THAT IF WE DON'T DROP OUR PRICE, WE'LL LOSE THE SALE?

We don't try to get a discount from Apple when we buy any of their products. They've shown from the start that they stand for high quality products and providing an exceptional experience. It's part of the appeal and the price.

They've told us that they will not discount. Ever. And over time they've stood by this claim. In doing so, we've been conditioned to buy now, no waiting for the next sale. If we want an Apple product we will pay their price. End of story.

Now let's talk about Walmart. They are all about low prices. They have trained us to shop with them if we want to buy things on the cheap.

How about Nordstroms? They captured the market's eye years ago with their solid customer service. They empower their employees to do all they can to ensure a memorable experience for their shoppers.

Many articles have been written about them. There's even a book, *The Nordstrom Way,* which covers how their core values are the basis of their world class customer service.

All three of these businesses are successful. Yet they all stand for different things.

There are many more. Eileen Fisher, Zappos, White Castle and Pottery Barn. Each one brings to mind specific angles that they are known for. Nobody questions them. It's just the way it is.

What about you? Who are you and what does your business stand for?

Have you ever thought about it? Not sure?

If you are all over the board on price and position, you don't stand for anything. It's time to claim a position.

But no worries, there is no time like the present. Make a stand and stay consistent with it.

Chapter 19

PENNY CANDY

———————~———————

Penny was in heaven. Her dream of opening a bath shop had come true.

To her amazement, Soapy Scents was going better than she could have possibly imagined. She sold online so her overhead was low. For that reason, Penny decided she could price her products low too and beat out any competition.

It was working! She had so many orders she could barely keep up. Her sister started helping out with the shipping.

Since she had to replenish her inventory regularly, she could buy wholesale in larger quantities. She even negotiated a better rate due of her volume. With this lower rate, she reduced her prices even further to make a statement and get even more business.

Orders were increasing as she anticipated, and her revenue was going up, up, up! That prompted Penny to start thinking about opening Soapy Scents franchises.

Wow! This small business life is great!

Fast forward six months and Penny is not thinking the same way. Oh, don't get me wrong, the sales continue to roll in. Soapy Scents is trending to bring in over $250,000 this year.

So, where's the problem?

The costs to run the business far outweigh the sales coming in. If she keeps going the way she is, Penny will have $350,000 in costs and only $250,000 in sales. She'll be in the red by $100,000. This is not part of the plan.

What happened?

It all points back to the pricing strategy Penny implemented in the beginning.

When she priced her product, she looked only at the primary cost to sell her soaps. She didn't consider any of the hidden or indirect costs.

Let me explain in more detail. When she purchased handmade soap bars at $1.25 each, she decided to sell them at $2.00. This was following her low-price strategy. She was thinking she made 75 cents on each bar.

She forgot about the shipping costs to get the soap bars to her. Then there was the order processing, packaging and shipping to her customers ... not to mention the costs of running the business overall.

She completely ignored the costs associated with website development, marketing and advertising. And purchasing software programs needed for accounting, inventory management, etc.

You might note I didn't even mention a salary for Penny and her sister. Yikes!

Pricing your product is a make or break decision. You need to look at the whole picture. Be very aware of all your costs and decide on a pricing strategy accordingly.

For creators specifically, there is a tendency to underprice or not charge at all for production time. That's a dangerous decision.

I've said it before, but I want to emphasize it again.

Your skill and talent comes so naturally to you that it's easy to under-estimate its value.

Additionally, you invest in tools or equipment to make your art. You take classes to learn advanced techniques. You may even attend conferences to stay up to date on your craft. This makes your time and expertise worth money.

There is a lot of information available about pricing. Consult our friend, Google, for all the details you need. Search specifically for pricing in your particular industry and product.

This book is not intended to focus on the details of setting your price. But, I would be remiss in not bringing up the potential downfall that business owners make.

It can lead to closed doors and high debt very quickly. I don't want that to happen to you.

Chapter 20

LESS IS SO MUCH MORE

———— ∼ ————

Picture this. You own a retail shop. Customers come in and spend time looking around. They handle the products on the shelves and then walk out the door.

OR

You're selling products at a farmer's market. People look at what you have displayed, touch a few of the items or take sample after sample and then walk away.

You're screaming under your breath.

What's wrong? You've come so close to buying my product. Why did you stop and walk away?

Is it possible that you are offering too many choices?

Where you would think having more options would bring you more sales, many times it's actually a hindrance to the sale.

WHERE YOU WOULD THINK HAVING MORE OPTIONS WOULD BRING YOU MORE SALES, MANY TIMES IT'S ACTUALLY A HINDRANCE TO THE SALE.

Experiments show that people become overwhelmed when presented with too many choices. Even more importantly, it affects their decision about whether to buy.

Take this example conducted by Sheena Iyengar of Columbia University. A table of Wilkin and Sons Jams was displayed outside a grocery store in Menlo Park, CA for two consecutive Saturdays. They tested the results of offering six flavors or 24 flavors to see how it affected sales.

The results prove the case for fewer product options. When 24 flavor options were displayed, 60% of the people who passed by stopped to sample but only 3% purchased. When there were only six flavor options available, 40% of the people stopped yet 30% purchased!

That's a pretty solid case for fewer options.

Wendy from Pinzit will confirm this too. Her fashion accessory at one time came in 40 different designs. But she could see that the people who stopped by at craft shows were overwhelmed. They struggled to choose which one to buy and sometimes that meant they bought nothing.

As a result, she narrowed down her selection to 10 designs that were the best sellers.

As an aside, this also makes producing her product through an outside manufacturer much more realistic. This is a necessity if she wants to grow her business.

So, what should you do if you have too many sweaters in your store?

Trim down the options to six of the best-selling seasonal trending colors and styles.

If there are too many chocolate flavor options at your trade shows reduce down to the three best sellers and see how it affect sales.

Here's an idea if you have too many spice mix varieties on your website. Combine mixes into themed packages such as Holiday Baking or Italian Cuisine. That way you can reduce the number of actual products while still offering all the flavors.

This can be particularly effective to clear out inventory as you switch to a less-is-more strategy.

Refine, combine or limit your product offerings and see how that attracts customers and prompts them to purchase.

I want you saying, "Thank you, come again." Not "Wait! Come back. Why didn't you buy?"

Chapter 21

TIS THE SEASON

———————~———————

You took a risk on a new product that you thought for sure your customers would love. You've sold a couple. But the rest have been sitting around for a few months.

Don't beat yourself up about it. You have to suffer through some bad purchases in order to see the reward from the real winners.

As you become familiar with what your customers want, your winners will far outweigh your losers.

But you don't want to keep those loser products in inventory for too long. They take up space. And if they aren't selling, having them on the sales floor for any length of time makes your shop look dated.

Retain too much stale inventory and overall your sales will start to decline.

Here are ideas on how to clear out the old stuff.

In-Store Sale. This one is obvious. Discount the product to see if it moves. Start at cost or slightly above and if it doesn't clear out, drop the price even below what you paid for it. Getting some money back is better than keeping the product in inventory indefinitely.

Sidewalk Sales. This is different than an in-store sale. Sidewalk Sales usually have multiple stores' participation. It may be a downtown community of shops or a strip mall. These events will attract a larger crowd and bring in people other than your regular customer.

Many retailers use this as a way to clear out their shop. Products that don't sell are taken off the floor and specifically held for this purpose. If you have storage space, it's a great option.

Online Sales. For items that you can't turn no matter what you do, try posting them on eBay. If you have only one or two pieces left or an incomplete set of something, this is a way to get it out the door.

Clearing out those loser and miscellaneous products will allow the dollars spent on them to be off your mind and in your bank account.

There is beauty in stocking the right products, claiming a price position and ensuring your products are priced with a healthy yet fair margin. Your business will start to grow.

And as you do, there will come a time when you'll need to bring in help. Almost every successful business owner says they wish they would have done it sooner.

Maybe it's the unknown of how to handle employees that causes the delay. For sure it's the fear of being responsible for someone else's paycheck.

I can't wait to share with you how this can be much less intimidating than it initially seems.

You may be in a position to hire right now. Check out the upcoming "Free and Mighty" section to see what I mean.

Employees

RUBBING SHOULDERS

No question about it. When you bring in others to work with you, it gets more complicated. But it also has its perks.

You can hire someone to take over responsibilities you struggle to complete. There is a thought exchange which can lead to improved systems and new ideas. There is a world of benefits that come with the addition of employees.

How do you find the right people though? And once you've got someone good, how can you keep them long-term?

Chapter 22

IT'S NOT ABOUT THEM

———————~———————

H iring is one of the most stressful and difficult things a business owner does.

This holds true for all companies but particularly us; the Gifters-Bakers-Crafters-Makers.

We have a bonded personal connection to our products.

How could you possibly allow someone else to make your custom-designed rings? Or how could you be so vulnerable as to let someone do your bookkeeping and see your financial reports?

I get it. I've been there. But if you want to grow past a certain point, you have to bring on people to help you.

Once you've bought into this inevitability, the next step is to find the right person. This is another point where people run into serious trouble.

Cynthia knows this only too well. She owns a boutique gift shop in Savannah. The products in her shop are sold on consignment and represent the creations of over 50 artisans from Georgia and South Carolina.

In selling on consignment, an artist displays their pieces in Cynthia's boutique. If a piece is sold, the money is split between the two parties.

Her shop became a "go to" place drawing people from miles away. There was so much traffic, the front door had to be propped open by a large porcelain urn. It didn't make sense for it to open and close every other second.

Day after day, Cynthia ran from one person to another, attending to the long line of customers wanting to purchase. She also had to immediately register the sale to the right artisan so she didn't lose track.

She was barely keeping up.

In stepped a savior. Veronica was a long-time friend of Cynthia's. She was recently laid off from her job as a school district administrator.

She offered to come work at the shop and explained how it would be a great solution for both of them. She was looking for work and Cynthia needed help.

This sounded perfect. Veronica had professional experience from her prior position and Cynthia was desperate.

The problem was that Veronica did not have the skills to do the required work. What was a challenging situation became a nightmare.

Purchases were being applied to the wrong artisans. Even worse, customers were not getting answers to their questions which resulted in frustrated people walking out the door.

The porcelain urn was no longer needed.

Both Cynthia and Veronica were miserable and there was serious tension in the friendship.

What started out as a good solution for both sides turned toxic.

Cynthia learned her lesson the hard way.

What can we learn from this?

Make sure to hire for the skills required in a position. Don't reverse this process and try to fit the position to one specific person.

Here's an additional tip. Many say that you should never hire friends or family. I think it depends.

My most valuable hire came to me as a friend first. She convinced me why she should come on board. Shout out to Lauri, I don't know what I'd do without you.

Chapter 23

DOING IT YOUR WAY

Have you ever been in a position where someone is looking over your shoulder watching every move you make?

If so you know it's not fun. Your blood pressure increases and you actually perform worse than if you were left unattended.

"The gingerbread cookies need to go in that gift basket before you add the coffee wafers."

"Don't tie the bow from underneath. You need to loop the strands over the top first."

Jessica was a dedicated and reliable production manager for a large gift basket business. She was responsible for a team of 14 people who put together the gift baskets. They were shipped all over the world and the company was known for their quality and upscale design of the finished gift.

Jessica took great pride in the number of gifts her team produced each hour. It was rare that any of her gifts got caught in quality control for rework either.

When teams competed on production numbers, she was always at the top of the list. But there was a problem.

Turnover on her team was higher than any of the other five groups. People continually reported to human resources to be reassigned. Or they just quit.

Jessica was so rigid in the management of her people that they worked in fear. Fear of being publicly critiqued. Fear of not living up to the quality expected. Fear of just not being "good enough."

Exit interviews revealed a common question. "If I can produce the same product in the end but get there in a different way because it's easier for me, why can't I do it my way? I feel stifled and unhappy here."

Jessica meant well. But it was her way of achieving results that wasn't working. This became a drain on the business. Continually replacing and training people cost the company money.

The story ends well. Jessica went through an employee relations course and learned a valuable lesson. She finally understood what her past interactions did to her team members.

She learned that there was so much more to her job than having the most gift baskets produced each hour.

She came back to work after training with a whole new plan.

Jessica met with her team and explained what she learned in her course. First, she shared what drove her to act as she had and how proud she was with their output numbers each week. Then she talked about what she sees should change.

She explained that she now understands the effect her words and actions had on them. As humbling as it was for her, she admitted there was a better way.

Right then and there she gave her team permission to build the gift baskets in whatever way was most comfortable for them. The only stipulation was it had to result in the same design and quality the company was known for.

What happened? Her team continued to produce the highest numbers and there were zero defections. In fact, her team became the model to which others strived to achieve.

Much to Jessica's surprise, she liked her job more too. The interaction between her and her team was more comfortable, supportive and enjoyable. She found that she didn't need to be in tight control of every little thing. That eased the pressure she put on herself.

Jessica learned that as the leader, you need to allow those who work with you the ability to take ownership of a task and to complete it in their own way.

Pride in a job well done and having the responsibility for its success are important small wins for your employees each and every day.

PRIDE IN A JOB WELL DONE AND HAVING THE RESPONSIBILITY FOR ITS SUCCESS ARE IMPORTANT SMALL WINS FOR YOUR EMPLOYEES EACH AND EVERY DAY.

Chapter 24

A KIND WORD OR GESTURE

———— ~ ————

Employee retention is a big deal. When you finally find that perfect person, how do you ensure that they stay with you for as long as possible?

As a small business trying to grow, you can't increase salaries over and over again. Yes, the money is important but there is so much more to keeping an employee than that.

Research shows that most people stay with a company because of relationships. Job satisfaction also catapults up to 50% when an employee has friends at work.

This benefits the employer and the employee.

"Work serves a social purpose for most people; we enjoy socializing and simply spending time with people whom we like and trust. In addition to making time at work more enjoyable, it also impacts people's commitment to their jobs and colleagues, which positively impacts effort and performance," says Casey Mulqueen, Ph.D., Director of Research for a Colorado-based workplace performance company.

Fortunately, there are things you can do that don't cost a dime and lead to fulfillment and satisfaction for your employees.

As the leader, you set the tone for your business. When people arrive, do you greet them with a smile? Do you take an interest in their personal life and the things that are important to them outside of the shop? Do you recognize birthdays or other special significant occasions? All these offer an opportunity to show you care about them as a person not just an employee.

When people feel valued and appreciated, they develop an emotional attachment that is more important than money. This is key to keeping employees for the long term.

WHEN PEOPLE FEEL VALUED AND APPRECIATED, THEY DEVELOP AN EMOTIONAL ATTACHMENT THAT IS MORE IMPORTANT THAN MONEY.

During my high school years, I worked in a popular women's clothing store. It was a great job for a teenage girl.

I'm still not sure what percentage of my paycheck went to clothes versus the savings my parents expected. But that's an aside.

I turned down a management position to go to college. But when I returned for winter or summer breaks, they always wanted me to come in and work. And I did. I loved it there.

It wasn't the standing on my feet all day or even the paycheck. It was being able to interact with my friends who worked there and to see past customers. It felt like home.

This is how you want your employees to feel too.

It won't work for every business. But today quality of life work scheduling is popular.

If you have a position where tasks need to be completed on a deadline, but they don't need to take place at a certain time of day, flex hours are great. Allow employees to work when they want as long as a project is completed on time.

This also pertains to the option of working from home. Posting on social media, writing newsletters and customer service calls can be done off-location. This adds to an employee's lifestyle.

Positive work environments, flexible scheduling and the ability to work from home are all no-cost attractive options for that perfect employee.

Here's something even easier. Recognize and verbally reward a job well done. The simple act of saying thank you or pointing out how much you appreciate a job well done is worth millions!

Chapter 25

EVEN WHEN YOU LIKE THEM

———⌒———

"**M**om loves me more."
"No, she doesn't. I'm her favorite."

If you have brothers and sisters I'm sure this debate came up over the morning bowl of Frosted Flakes or a long car ride to the zoo. It may even linger to this day.

Like siblings, your employees will compare themselves to each other. Be aware of how you treat them, so you don't create perceived inequity.

Subtle undertones of discontent can affect productivity. Even worse, it can poison the vibe given off to customers.

Have you ever walked into a store and overheard a conversation full of complaining and negativity between co-workers? It's uncomfortable, awkward and not a place you want to stay in for too long.

Following some simple steps can help set the tone for a new employee right from the start. When everyone goes through the same process, you're showing base-level equality.

I say base level because when there are different positions within a company, the interactions will vary simply by nature of the roles.

For example, take a sales person versus a manager. Each will have access to different systems and knowledge about different aspects of the business. The discussions you have with each will vary too. But the overriding principles that drive the business and how you treat people can still be the same.

It's a good idea to have a list of the top company values posted in the work or break room for all to see. This makes your commitment more formal and stands as a reminder for everyone.

When a new employee comes onboard, have them sign a Non-Disclosure Agreement (NDA). Yes, even a part-time high school employee.

These agreements signify that you expect confidential information to remain private.

Of course, many employees will never be exposed to this type of information. But having them sign an NDA establishes trust. It also makes a statement that they are now an important member of the organization.

Depending on your business, you may also want an employee to sign a non-compete. This is significant if you have a business where an employee could go off later and start a competitive company.

If they gain knowledge from working with you that could advance their business farther than what they could have done starting on their own, then it would be wise to look into this protection.

Employees are the greatest asset you have. Without them you can't make progress. I cannot overstate how important it is that they work harmoniously and feel rewarded and fulfilled with their jobs.

Matt Holmes knows this well. In fact, investing in his employees is one of the major focuses of his business. Home & Company is a gift and decor store in Holland, MI.

Matt believes selling is a skill that can be taught. They have a formal process and work one-on-one with each employee to develop these skills.

The result is a loyal staff who know they are valued, feel confident in their roles and stay at Home & Company for years.

Sounds pretty perfect, doesn't it?

Chapter 26

FREE AND MIGHTY

―――――――〜―――――――

Here's a gem of an opportunity to get help in your business that is often overlooked. Interns!

Particularly when you are starting out but even when you are up and running strong, keep this option in your back pocket.

The beauty of an internship is that both sides benefit and are motivated to make it work.

I'm talking here specifically about free internships but you can create a paid internship as well.

The advantage for you is having a temporary employee who is up to speed with the latest information and newest techniques.

Interns are at a point in their education or career where there is incentive to prove they can put their skills to work.

Junior and Senior high school students will highlight their internship on college applications. Practical, real-world experience can be the tipping point for getting an offer to their top school or not.

On your side, you can get projects completed that you may not have the time or an employee with the skills to accomplish.

Interns are perfect for tasks such as social media posting and overall management, logo creation, photography, website development and more.

Project specific programs work best. The intern should be able to show completion of a task during the time they are with you. They need to be able to take away a solid result and learned skills that they can use going forward.

Finding interns is easy and can be done year-round. Contact your local high school and even a community college for applicants.

Before you do, however, have a clear description of what the project is. It should include a timeframe, skills required, time and place for work to be done and any other necessary details.

When you hire an intern, there should be some type of reporting involved. If it's a formal internship the school will provide a report to complete. These are used to officially document that said person did work for you in an intern role.

It will include how satisfied you were with the results and any other comments on their performance. If a form isn't provided, you can provide all the same information in a letter upon their completion of the job.

Remember, they are using the internship to advance themselves. You are providing a learning experience in exchange for their investment of time and expertise.

As a final note, there are a couple of other benefits you can realize from an intern.

If your customer base is young, you may see your sales increase. An intern will tell his/her friends about their job and potentially promote your business to them.

Also, if your intern's experience with you is exceptional, you may be looking at a new employee for the future.

Interns. An opportunity just waiting for you to tap into.

Fulfilling interpersonal relationships are the key to stable and long-lasting employee experiences.

I'm sure you can look back over your years of employment and find both good and bad examples.

Remember how you felt in these instances. It can help guide you as you make your workplace as rewarding an environment as possible.

Positive interactions need to happen with another group of people as well. Your customers!

You may be shocked to hear the position I take here. I'll be wondering if you agree.

Customers

———— ～ ————

LET'S BE FRIENDS

Do you have a hair stylist that you can't wait to see every time you get your hair done? Or do you cringe when you go to get your morning coffee and see that it's the sour-faced barista making your drink?

How you interact with customers can make or break repeat business and your reputation.

But at the same time, you should not be a slave to our customers either.

In the best scenario it's give and take, as any relationship should be.

Let's dive into how to turn someone into a loyal supporter of your business.

We'll also talk about when it's time for some customers to hit the road. Yes, I said it!

Chapter 27

I FEEL SPECIAL

⁓

Have you ever entered a room and immediately felt at home? The colors, the style, the very vibe of the space invokes happiness and you feel at peace and nurtured.

For me this special place is miles away on the Jersey Shore. I have a dear friend who lives there. I get such a kick out of all the Monopoly themed street names. Marvin Gardens was always my favorite property. Actually, I think Monopoly properties are named after that area, not the other way around.

Anyway, Jennifer has a beautiful home right on the water with two outside decks. I can't explain why but the top deck is where I find my peace. In fact, a good portion of this book was written there.

I open the sliding door and set up on the white wooden bar-height round table. The blue striped cushioned chair is perfect because when I put my feet on the lower slat, my back is in a comfortable position and I can work for hours. This is all before I even look out into the bay.

To the right is the Margate Bridge that rises up intermittently to let in a big ship. The seagulls land periodically to check in on me and the tide goes in and out with all its mysterious glory.

I have no idea why I'm so productive there. But I can crank out work like crazy. It is definitely one of my "happy places."

What if your customers felt like this when they visited your store or your website? What if they felt connected and pampered because what you offer is what they love? The colors, the atmosphere and the message align with them so deeply they can't resist another visit.

Or they get lost in your website traveling from page to page discovering one beautiful image after another.

You didn't know you can do this with websites? Check out Nicole's site at Cedar and Rush. This is definitely guilty pleasure time for me. I want to be in those pictures. I want to own many of those products.

This works because Nicole knows her customer so well. She's niched her business down specifically to that audience. Those who resonate with her brand are passionate about it.

You can do this too. Whether you have a brick and mortar shop or an online business, think about why people are attracted to you. Then ensure that your business "spaces" cater to your audience and make them feel at home and special.

ENSURE YOUR BUSINESS "SPACES" CATER TO YOUR AUDIENCE AND MAKE THEM FEEL AT HOME AND SPECIAL.

Time in your space plus emotional connection equals sales.

Chapter 28

I WANT TO KNOW YOU

———— ∼ ————

The money is in the list. This is a common statement of online marketing gurus. It's true not just for them though.

An email list is an asset for every company. It's through your email list that you can stay in touch with prospects and customers.

It's important here to differentiate between email lists and social media followers. I don't want you to feel a false sense of security and pass up this section on emails because you're thinking about the 8,624 followers you have on your business Facebook Page.

These are two completely different things.

An email list is a business asset that you own. Nobody can take those contacts away from you unless someone opts out of your list. You can talk to your email connections any time you want and rest easy knowing they are a growing asset that will be there tomorrow.

Regardless of the platform, social media followers are not people you can communicate with except on that platform. What if Facebook changes their rules (yet again) or worse yet, your account gets shut down? If that were to happen, you lose all contact with every single follower you had.

This has happened to people I know. Facebook jail is a real thing and some never get out. Which means they had to start all over again.

Sure, you can rebuild your followers, but you're building a house on sand. It can all be washed away again, and the devastation is completely out of your control.

But your email list is a treasure. If you were to sell your business someday, there are real dollars exchanged for the quality and quantity of a company's email list.

Best practices are to capture emails and separate them into categories based on different variables. Some systems call this tagging.

You can tag people as being customers or prospects. You can tag them by what products they buy, if they took advantage of a special offer, or if they only purchase during the busy holiday season.

Separating and tagging is important. It allows you to write emails worded so they relate specifically to that audience. Your email recipients then feel like you are talking directly to them.

But it all starts with having an email list in the first place.

Let's talk about ways you can collect email addresses. Here are some ideas:

- Website newsletter signup
- Free raffles at checkout in your store
- When they place an order online
- Event specific drawings like sidewalk sales
- Business cards you exchange at networking events (not in bulk but individually)

I'm sure you can add your own magic sprinkles to this list and easily double it.

To make it legal, you must clearly state somewhere that when they provide their email, they are giving you permission to communicate with them.

Even if you're not sure what you will do with the emails you capture, start collecting them today.

Every email contact you pass up is a lost sales opportunity for the future.

Chapter 29

ALWAYS RIGHT? NOT!

———————～———————

A restaurant in my community has a sign behind the register that reads:

"There is only one boss. The customer. He can fire everybody in the company from the chairman on down simply by spending his money somewhere else."

A customer has the right to be a patron of the establishment of their choice. But I don't think that a customer is always right. As business owners, we should not sacrifice our company values or be taken advantage of in order to retain a customer.

WE SHOULD NOT SACRIFICE OUR COMPANY VALUES OR BE TAKEN ADVANTAGE OF IN ORDER TO RETAIN A CUSTOMER.

A disgruntled customer should always be heard and understood. But there are times when you need to stand your ground in a friendly and compassionate way.

Acceptance of your position by the customer in most cases will be determined by the way you phrase your comments. You always want to show that you value a customer's business and you never want to insult their character. Arguments get you nowhere.

Here are some situations when you should stand your ground.

Actions that go against your company policies or principles. At The Ribbon Print Company, we have a policy that we treat all customers equally. I believe trust and loyalty results from consistent actions and expectations.

For example, our proprietary software is highly guarded. We have bolted down security on it with good reason. People have tried to steal our code. Luckily our system is solid, but expensive.

It's our policy that the software is only accessible to the first owner of a ribbon printer. If that printer is sold, the software does not transfer over to a second buyer. They need to purchase it themselves.

This is also because of the level of support we provide and the commitment that when we update the program, all existing users get the updates at no extra charge.

We honor this policy completely. That way anyone who sells or buys a ribbon printer will have the same experience.

Imagine if someone bought a used machine and found out later that someone else didn't need to buy the software. It would result in bitterness and a loss of trust that would be hard to win back.

Unreasonable requests. I don't think customers always intend to be unreasonable. They just aren't informed about the hoops you need to jump through to fill their request.

Many requests are outside of what you do as a business in the first place. And customers want it done at no charge of course.

This is a danger zone. You may be tempted to help a customer, but it will drain time and resources. It could also produce an undesirable result because it's not what you're in business to do.

I urge you not to be swayed into doing anything and everything to save one client. It drains your time and energy. You are then losing opportunities to service your ideal customer.

If a request is not in your area of expertise, the best approach is to explain why you cannot agree to the customer's idea. If possible, point them in the direction of someone who can help.

Abusive behavior. If a customer gets abusive with their language or physically abusive, it's over. Period.

In the end, whether you sell a product or provide a service it's all about relationships.

As much as you want to please everyone, you should not be taken advantage of because you own a business and the customer should always be right.

If you've done everything reasonable and your customer is still complaining, then maybe it's just not a good match.

That's the time to respectfully part ways and move on.

Chapter 30

IT'S OVER

———⌇———

I t's sad but sometimes it has to be done. You have to fire a customer.

I hear you saying, "What? And lose out on the sales from that customer?"

The answer is yes. And it's better for you in the long run.

There are times when you and a customer are just not the right fit.

Here are some examples of when this is the case.

Lack of skills to use the product or service. Using The Ribbon Print Company as an example again, one only needs basic computer skills to use the system.

However, there have been times when we'll get a customer who doesn't know how to save a file. Or there will be someone who doesn't understand you need to double click to open a program.

In this case, we suggest they find a basic computer class and come back to us once they've completed their training. We are not in the business of teaching someone how to use a computer.

Out of bounds employee interactions. I've experienced situations where a customer is unreasonable. They continue to show frustration for a product that isn't made to do what they want it to do. Or they refuse to follow our suggestions for troubleshooting. Then they continue to get a poor outcome because they aren't using the product as it's intended.

Understandably this results in frustration. But when it escalates to insults, swearing or name calling, it's time to end the conversation.

If this type of behavior continues in the next interaction, my team knows they should explain that we don't communicate in that way and will need to stop doing business together.

Personal, health or emotional issues. Life happens. Sometimes our customers are thrown curveballs that prevent them from making progress with a project or goal. This usually applies to services such as coaching or time-sensitive training programs.

Sometimes customers don't even recognize themselves that the best course of action is to delay or stop work altogether. You can always pick up again when the situation gets better.

In the end, doing what is right for your employees and your customers can be a fine line. Sometimes tough decisions need to be made.

Chapter 31

WAIT ... WHAT?

————————∽————————

Why do we sit behind a closed door trying to anticipate what our customers want?

We strategize for hours on which promotion will get them excited to buy. Or which new style scarf would be the best pattern for class.

Guess what? There's an easier way to do this.

Ask them. Ask your customer what they want.

Then go a step past asking. Really hear what they are telling you and the messages they are giving you.

They will hand you information on the proverbial silver platter. They'll give you answers to all your questions that tell you exactly how to grow your business.

Sometimes what they say is obvious. But other times, it will surprise you.

For Ryann, it led to a complete repositioning of her company.

Gaspara Flora started out with a focus on providing hotel welcome gifts for weddings. Being in San Diego, she's in a prime location for destination weddings and surrounded by lots of venues she could approach for business.

As she presented her concept to big hotels and boutique inns, she started to see a common pattern in their responses. They loved her product but looked at it for more than weddings. They were interested in using her products for corporate gifts instead.

This was not what Ryann expected. But being the savvy business owner that she is, she listened and truly heard the underlying need that her product could fill.

It didn't take long for Ryann to pivot her business focus to corporate gifting. That resulted in sales naturally coming her way.

All you have to do is look online at the beautiful gifts she creates and the businesses she's working with. You'll see what a wise choice she made.

If she had not been attentive and listened to what her prospects were telling her, she probably would still have had a stable business. But nothing like what she has today.

Not all customer ideas need to result in as dramatic a shift as Ryann's. But you might discover new product options. Or there may be new paid service opportunities.

A new income steam or system improvement is always worth discovering. These lead to new customers and new sales.

And it all begins by listening.

We've just covered how to turn customers into advocates of your brand. The good, the bad and the ugly.

But how do you get these customers in the first place?

The good news is you have lots of options here!

Getting Business

COME VISIT

Tony's Subs is always jam packed with people. Claire's salon hardly ever has availability for walk-in manicures. Jessica's craft fair table is so packed with people you never get a chance to say "hi."

There's a secret to making this happen. It is not one thing you do that magically attracts customers. It's a number of things done regularly that creates a steady flow of faces into your store or viewers landing on your website.

You can pick and choose which ones feel best to you or switch them up as you wish.

Chapter 32

ONE PLUS ONE

---~---

When you first enter the business world, you start making connections and building your circle of contacts - your network.

If you are an established business owner, you already have a network. It may be small or large depending on your time in business and how much you've been out and about.

Connections form through networking meetings and participating in events in your community. They also form by attending conferences and trade shows.

They are customers, vendors, fellow business owners in your community, as well as peers within your industry.

As you learn more and more about the people you meet, you may discover that they need services others in your network provide.

Connecting two people together for their mutual benefit is a powerful business activity, even though there is no obvious advantage for you.

CONNECTING TWO PEOPLE TOGETHER FOR THEIR MUTUAL BENEFIT IS A POWERFUL BUSINESS ACTIVITY, EVEN THOUGH THERE IS NO OBVIOUS ADVANTAGE FOR YOU.

When you help connect others, your professional and personal reputation rises.

Going into a conversation with the idea of identifying ways you can help others leads to interesting discussions too.

It will get you past the boring "Hello, what do you do?" introduction.

Why not talk about business successes, today's challenges or common thoughts on business strategy? These discussions are so much more rewarding than boring expected niceties.

When meeting someone for the first time, the purpose of your conversation is not to sell. It is to understand *their* business and how you can help them.

Your relationships will grow over time. That's why repetitive networking is important. As you see the same people again and again, a bond and level of trust develops. This results in both parties being more likely to open up and share.

A friend comes to mind as a great example. Years ago, she was one of my sales associates. Kris was a top performer and model employee. She had something else really special too. Something she still has today.

Her network is huge and growing all the time. She understands the power of connecting people who can use the assistance of another to advance their business.

Over the years Kris has worked at several companies and continues to be a star. She advances by her choice and regularly gets offers to consider new opportunities.

Sometimes it's because one of her managers leaves and wants to take her with them. Other times it's a client who wants to hire her because they recognize her skills and strong track record.

What has always stood out to me with Kris is her ability to unselfishly connect people together for their common good. She is exceptional in this area and I know this has a lot to do with the high level of success she has today.

Creating a reputation like Kris has is the goal of networking. Doors open easily, and opportunities present themselves when you're not even looking.

Chapter 33

LET'S BE SOCIAL

———⌇———

Facebook, Instagram, Twitter, Pinterest, LinkedIn and on and on. By the time you're reading this who knows what new platform will appear.

Like it or not, social media is here to stay.

It presents the ability for us to reach out and be seen like never before.

The power comes in its worldwide access. Where once you were limited to customers in your local area or the subscribership of a newspaper, today you can do business almost anywhere.

It's even more useful in the ability to narrow down to your specific audience and speak to them directly.

There are also communities that have formed within the whole. Facebook Groups, Hashtag Hubs and Twitter Chats exist where people gather online and talk. Many of these communities are free to join and the conversations are detailed and helpful because they pertain specifically to the topic of the group.

If you're looking for a group to join to see what this is all about, jump over to my free Facebook group at Gift Biz Breeze.

Help centers are also set up within Facebook. Companies provide clients a place to go when they need troubleshooting or other types of assistance.

At The Ribbon Print Company, we have a private Facebook group for the owners of our systems. It is an active place with photos being shared, questions asked, successes celebrated, and friendships made.

Since it's a private group, there are things discussed that only those in the group can see.

That allows for an elevated level of trust and camaraderie.

If someone is having trouble with a customer, they can present the problem there. If someone is unclear on how they should price a job, they'll hear from others who share what they do. And it's a resource if they are having difficulty running the printer. Help is there from fellow system owners as well as our customer service team.

Check out groups for your industry or groups around a special product you use. You may have to request to join and answer a few questions to get in. But once inside, you'll find a community of people with detailed conversations worth your time.

If it's not the right group for you, or it's a spammy group with everyone selling their stuff, leave and go find another group.

Or maybe you want to start a group of your own!

Information abounds about all the different social media channels along with strategies on how best to get results from each one.

Here are topline best practices that transcend the individual sites. They are important when you want to see positive results regardless of the platform.

Open a Business Account. If you are using social media for business, you need a business account where it is offered.

In most cases, having a business account is the only way to see statistics or run ads. Again, things change so fast who knows what else may apply only to business accounts at the time you're reading this.

Start with two platforms. If you are opening your business now, pick one or two platforms to get started. They should be the ones your ideal customer (your avatar) is using so you can get in front of them. Most likely it will be Facebook and one other.

It's easy to get swayed into thinking you are missing something if you aren't on the latest platform that appears. Don't succumb to the idea that you have to be on all social media platforms right away ... or ever.

Define your strategy. Each social media platform has its own unique strength and audience. Therefore, your business goals should vary too. Determine what you expect from your participation on each site. Then watch your stats to see if your posting schedule and content are actually producing those results.

Word your posts for your audience. Remember to speak to your ideal customer when creating the wording on your posts. Many people get confused here. They direct their photos and wording to friends, peers or to appease their ego.

Ask yourself what your ideal customer would want to see. What is it that will deepen their relationship with you and your business? This is what you post. For more information on this go back and review the examples in the "Hi! I Know You!" section.

One final comment here on social media. Please don't make the mistake of thinking an account on Facebook or Pinterest can replace a website of your own.

DON'T MAKE THE MISTAKE OF THINKING AN ACCOUNT ON FACEBOOK OR PINTEREST CAN REPLACE A WEBSITE OF YOUR OWN.

Because you don't own social media platforms, you don't have access to details about your followers or subscribers. If any platform changes their rules or goes away, you are left without the ability to contact those customers or prospects. All the work you put forth would be for nothing.

We talk about how to protect yourself from this in the "I Want to Know You" section.

The primary purpose of social media platforms is to attract and serve your customers.

Yes, you can sell there too. But if you don't provide content they find valuable, they'll leave.

Chapter 34

A COFFEE CHAT

———⌇———

One of the most intimidating things about networking is the dreaded elevator speech. This is where you get up in front of a room of people and introduce yourself and your business.

Scary! I completely get it.

But no need to worry, I've got you covered.

It does not have to be hard when you know what to say.

Most people make the mistake of trying to cover every little thing about their business in this 30-second time allotment.

Who cares about the address of your store? Tell me something that will peak my curiosity and make me want to find out more.

TELL ME SOMETHING THAT WILL PEAK MY CURIOSITY AND MAKE ME WANT TO FIND OUT MORE.

Let's talk about how to do this properly.

To start, the elevator speech needs a new name. I call it the Introduction Message.

Whew ... that doesn't sound so hard. Does it?

You want to cover some very basic information in your Introduction Message, so people understand what you do.

If it interests them, they will want to find out more. That's when they catch you after the meeting and start up a conversation.

I want you to follow a strategy I first heard from Amy Porterfield, someone I respect for her business savvy. She says, "Start simple, get fancy later."

So, let's start simple and I'll give you exactly what to say for your Introduction Message.

In fact, I've made it into a template. Just fill in your information and you're good to go.

Also, it's okay if you want to actually write it out and read from a piece of paper as you get going.

Listen, all of us have been in the same spot and can remember when we did our first public introduction. We can relate.

It's actually endearing to see someone step out of their comfort zone and take a risk. Trust me. You'll gain friends, not turn people away.

Here's your Introduction Message Template

Hi, I'm _____(name)_____, owner of _____ (your company) _____.

I help _____ (your customer description)_____ to____(result of your product/service)____.

That's it! That's all you need to say.

Again, as you get more comfortable and this slides off your tongue, you can add to it and "fancy" it up.

If you want more information on how to network with ease, check out how to get my Networking Ninja Course for free. Details are in the Resources section of this book.

Chapter 35

ONCE UPON A TIME

———— ~ ————

I'm wondering if you're like me. I have SO much trouble remembering names. Two seconds after I meet someone, I forget their name.

So embarrassing!

I've tried listening harder, repeating their name, everything. None of it worked.

Until I heard about a different system.

Now when I meet someone, I find something to relate to their name. I look for a differentiating physical trait or pick up something in a conversation we have and use that to remember their name.

For example, when I first met Karley, I remembered her name by associating it with her super curly hair. So Curly equals Karley. When I first met Bob, I remembered him because of his rather large nose. So Beak equals Bob. Gail wears crazy-looking glasses. Jackie has *just* one beauty mark on her face, and Mary is really good at math (she's an accountant).

I use these associations for names because it works. Now I can acknowledge people by name when I see them again.

Wouldn't it be fabulous if you could use a similar strategy in reverse? What if you could insure that people remember *you*?

This is possible through the power of telling stories.

Learning and using stories can be a game changer for your business.

When you tell a story, you've given people something not only to remember you by but also content to talk about when referencing you or your company.

You can use stories when you mingle at networking meetings, in creating posts for social media or when building rapport before presenting to a corporate client.

Now, I'm not talking about a story that goes on forever with side branches that lead to nowhere. I'm talking about glimpses into your life, your company, or you as a person.

It's so much better than the "Good morning. How are you?"

"Fine thank you. And you?"

"Doing well."

This is bland banter that goes absolutely nowhere.

What if this same encounter went something like this:

"Good morning. How are you doing today?"

"Great! My daughter's in town and we had dinner last night at Bluegrass. I love that restaurant. Have you ever been?"

"Of course, I love their Louisiana Blackened Grouper."

"Oh my gosh, that's exactly what I had last night. So good!"

See the difference?

The little dinner story was short and sweet. But it added personality and some friendly give and take to the conversation.

From there the chat can go elsewhere in a very comfortable way.

"I often take customers to Bluegrass when we celebrate a milestone."

"Oh really? What do you do by the way?"

And on and on … how different could your relationships be if they could get to this kind of conversation?

We miss so many opportunities with people we are around every day because we stay on the surface with boring expected verbal exchanges.

An important note here. People will like and remember you for stories and things that have nothing to do with your business too.

Don't be shy or think it's out of context to sprinkle in personal information. That's what makes you human.

We want to do business with people we are comfortable with and who we like. Stories make that happen.

Chapter 36

CAPTURE THE MOMENT

———— ～ ————

The here is nothing more powerful than word of mouth.

Once a friend tells you about her favorite handyman or the world's best dog groomer, do you even need to look further?

The reason referrals are so valuable is because the sale is almost already made. Referred prospects come to you with a favorable impression from the start. Your only job is to get them over the finish line.

YOUR ONLY JOB IS TO GET THEM OVER THE FINISH LINE.

So why do we struggle so much with asking for referrals? I know I do.

I think it's because I feel like I'm stepping over the invisible boundary of the customer relationship.

But I've found ways to get beyond that.

Set up a formal system. Create a referral system where the customer is rewarded for bringing other business your way. Many businesses are doing this these days so it's the easiest of all programs to institute. People are familiar and comfortable with the idea.

But make sure you remind your customers that the system exists. It's easy for them to forget about this option.

You can add a sentence to the bottom of an email. Include it on a customized sales receipt or print up a flyer that you include in their bag when they purchase. These are all ways to reinforce a referral program.

Capture in the moment. You can collect referrals directly or indirectly in the way of testimonials.

If you are at a trade show for example, and someone says something complimentary about your product, see if you can document it from your phone.

Many times, the hardest thing about testimonials is the wording. But after someone has already provided the words, you can play off that.

A video testimonial is the best but even if they only let you use their words attached to their name, you're set.

Bingo - a new testimonial is done within a couple of minutes!

Ask. I'll admit it, I'm not as good at this as I could be. But I'm working on it.

Once someone becomes a long-term and supportive client, I ask them if they know anyone else who could benefit from the product or service we offer. At this point, I feel like I'm at a level in the relationship where it won't jeopardize anything if I ask.

Some training programs suggest that you do this right after the sale. It may work. But I think it needs to happen a little further down the road. That's when a relationship is solid and the client has had an opportunity to experience what your product or service has to offer.

No matter which of these you put in place, or you create your own, make sure to take advantage of all the power referrals provide.

Chapter 37

POWER UP

———～———

P ower Partners. A golden opportunity that few people know about or take advantage of.

I'm so excited to share this with you because it has such great potential for bringing in more sales.

Let me back up.

A Power Partner is a complementary business that has a similar customer avatar but sells something different.

Here are some examples:

A dog trainer and the owner of a kennel.

A home organizer and a residential realtor.

A florist and a wedding photographer.

The value comes in working together and sharing each other's customers in a way that both participants benefit.

It's not just a win-win. It's a win-win-win. Each company gains visibility with new customers. And the customer wins by being introduced to new services that they may need.

Here are some examples of ways power partners can work together.

Combine products together and sell in two locations. Let's take a chocolate shop and a jeweler.

For Valentine's day they could work together to create a limited time product. It could include a heart chocolate truffle box and an *I Love You* charm necklace. They are packaged as one gift with a big red bow and have a predominant display in each shop.

The business owners determine the appropriate compensation division. No matter where a purchase is made, they split all sales according to that agreement.

Service/product combo. A hair salon could power partner with a hair accessories company.

There could be a weekend event in the salon demonstrating how to use the accessories. They could also teach customers right there how they can do it themselves.

Not only would people purchase for themselves, but they may tell their friends to go in and check it out.

This could work really well around the holidays or a high school dance. Who can resist glamming up their hair for those special occasions? If they have the hair products needed and know how to do it that is.

Service Packages. Combine services that are required to meet a common goal. The Power Partner concept does not need to be limited to only two companies.

In planning that once in a lifetime wedding, think of all the potential services involved. An event planner, florist, photographer, caterer, stationery store, DJ, videographer, hotel and limousine service are all possible partners.

Again, the idea is that your customers are the same but what you provide is different. This is why it works so well. You are not infringing or taking business from one another. You are enhancing each other's businesses.

Chapter 38

RSVP

T *he Only Holiday in August* is an event put on by Merley of Celebrate Sweetly. She has a gift basket business. At the end of the summer she gathers customers and other service or product providers together for a big bash.

It's perfect timing too. Corporate holiday plans are hitting the marketing departments "to do" lists right at that time. Contacts are made for party planning, employee appreciation and client holiday gifts.

Janet owns Alden's Kennels, an animal boarding and training facility in northern Illinois. She puts on a Multi-State Mixer in June that attracts business owners from miles away. It's no surprise that she draws such a crowd. Janet does it right.

She rolls out the red-carpet for all attendees. Literally people walk in on a red carpet.

Once inside, guests enjoy enticing food and beverages while mingling and listening to music. Sprinkled throughout the grounds are other entertaining activities too. This gives attendees plenty to experience and talk about as they meet new people.

It's THE networking event to attend. Notice it has nothing to do with pets and everything to do with introducing and connecting people.

Event marketing is an opportunity like no other. Bringing people together and providing a fun-filled experience reflects back on you. Events give you visibility with an audience you haven't reached before and provide a story to spread the word. We talked about the value of stories in the prior section, "Once Upon a Time."

EVENTS GIVE YOU VISIBILITY WITH AN AUDIENCE YOU HAVEN'T REACHED BEFORE AND PROVIDE A STORY TO SPREAD THE WORD.

Not all events need to be as lavish as these.

Brian of Lash L'Heureux outdid himself one year with Halloween decorations for a chamber sponsored business crawl. Word spread that you had to go and see his decor. That attracted people who had never been in Brian's salon before. Once they entered his location, they were one step closer to becoming a customer or making a referral.

Terri of My Secret Garden has regular get-togethers that attract customers into her store too. Moms, Muffins and Mimosas is one of my favorites in celebration of the start of a new school year. She also does in-store fashion shows highlighting the season's newest colors and styles.

Nick at Lucas Candies captures attention from customers and the media when he and Deb roll out their holiday handmade candy cane demonstrations. It's almost an impossible feat to make enough of these old-fashioned treats to meet demand.

Events are the way brick and mortar shops can compete with online stores.

Getting people into your space so they can see what you're all about is the biggest challenge. Events accomplish this.

All these customer acquisition options are based on you doing something to motivate your prospects to come to you.

Now let's talk about how you can go to them. There's a nice ring to that.

Did you know you can position yourself right in their line of vision? In a place where they are already in a mindset to hand over their credit card?

That's next.

Craft & Trade Shows

PLANS THIS WEEKEND?

When done right, local farmers markets, craft fairs and large trade shows provide the perfect venue to find new customers.

The great thing about these shows is they attract a crowd of people ... many you would never get in front of independently. You might also encounter someone who is looking for new items to carry in their shop, or even catch the eye of a large distributor.

You never know who will come by your booth. But one thing is certain. If you don't work the show in a professional manner, your sales opportunities will slip away. Many of them will never cross your path again.

Chapter 39

PSYCHOLOGY OF A SHOW

———————～———————

Local craft fairs exist in every part of the country. There are county fairs, community art show weekends and weekly local markets.

On the surface you might think that being at a craft show is a way to sell your product and make some extra money. Yes, it's that but oh so much more!

Let's talk about the other advantages you can realize from exhibiting at a show. After all, when you attend, you want to make the most out of it as possible.

Product Testing. Whether you're introducing your product for the first time or it's a new flavor you're adding to your product line, this is a great research center.

For the cost of entry, you have a focus group right in front of your eyes! Watch carefully and you can gain valuable information that will help direct your actions for the future. Consider things like:

Which flavors of your spice mix are the most popular?

What color candles are the biggest seller?

Do people understand what your product is right away, or do they need to see a demonstration?

Fairs also give you the opportunity to talk with people directly and gather additional market knowledge.

Maybe your vision is to sell on a global scale. Ask questions to determine what adjustments should be made to your product before you invest in a large amount of inventory.

Gain visibility. Yes, sales are important. It's always great to cover the costs of attending an event. But sales aren't everything.

You are getting visibility for your business even if someone doesn't buy right then and there. It's important to think of these shows in light of the future business they can create.

A potential customer may get distracted and will buy online later. Or they may remember you when they need a gift where your product is a perfect fit.

That is why the printed materials you have at your table are important and can play a big role.

Identify opportunities. Another advantage of craft shows is the interaction you have with the other exhibitors.

You can learn valuable information about the other shows they attend, how they developed their products or the contacts they have that could benefit you too. The potential is limitless.

You never know what you'll find until you start up a conversation and show interest in other people and their stories.

If you've ignored local craft shows before, I urge you to reconsider. They pave the way for the growth of your business.

One event builds upon another. People begin to expect your attendance and, in some cases, come to the show solely to see and buy from you.

That's a beautiful thing!

This is exactly what happens to Shenia of Lula's Bath and Bombs. There are lots of companies that make sugar scrubs and bath bombs, but not like she does.

People follow her from show to show to restock their supply and to see what new scents Shenia has concocted.

They also want to take in her dynamic spirited style. She has a way of interacting with her customers that's engaging and leaves you wanting more.

Chapter 40

CENTER OF ATTENTION

———～———

White smoke puffing out of a cauldron ...
A holiday tree dressed in colorful mittens ...

A turning rack with beveled beads that captures the light and reflects it off the opposite wall ...

Product displays that attract attention will also fill your pockets.

Not only do you effortlessly get people to check out your booth, you've provided them with something to talk about.

"You have to go check out the booth on the far wall. It's so cool!"

Use some creativity and give your booth style and pizazz for maximum attention and sales. Having an eye-catching booth does not mean it needs to be expensive.

Here are some things to consider as you design your next show display area.

Keep your product display simple and clean. Too much product can be overwhelming if it gets messy with people shuffling through everything. Make sure there's a nice balance between too much and too little.

Have signage that shows clear pricing. This is a question you'll have to answer over and over again if it's not clear. Or worse, people will walk away.

Display creatively. Instead of laying things out on a table, find more interesting ways to present your product. Think about using ladders, crates, wine racks or foliage. Search around online and you'll find lots of ideas to spark your creativity.

Make the atmosphere of your booth welcoming. This is done through color, layout of product, ample space for people to comfortably walk around, soft music playing ... and whatever else you can dream up. Your goal is for people to be so comfortable in your booth that they want to spend time and browse.

Perfecting your booth will be a work in progress. You can enhance your space over time as you see what is resonating and attracting a crowd and what you can do better.

Happy booth creation!

Chapter 41

IT'S A PARTY AND YOU'RE THE HOST

———— ～ ————

Whether you take part in a small local craft fair or a large trade show, think of your space as your party room. You are inviting people to your booth to talk and get to know you and see your products.

If this party were at your house, would you leave the door wide open and hope that people would come in without being invited? Would you see them and not greet them once they were inside?

I'm pretty sure you wouldn't. I'm also certain you wouldn't then disappear into another room and leave your guests on their own to entertain themselves.

So why would you do it in your booth?

Wait. Are you telling me you don't do that? Great, then I'll come to your party anytime!

Even so, I feel the need to go through some of the common mistakes people make when exhibiting at shows. It costs them a lot of sales.

Exhibitor Don'ts

- Sit focused on your phone when there are people in your booth.
- Leave your booth unattended with only literature to do the selling for you. What if they want to buy?
- Have a private party in your booth with your friends and ignore potential customers.
- Be non-responsive and show how tired you are ... even at the end of a long day ... smile!
- Start packing up early at the end of a show. Everyone who attends should have the ability to see a full display.

Exhibitor Do's

- Acknowledge someone's presence with a smile or nod if you're busy and can't interact with them right away.
- Be alert and available if you see that someone has a question but also let people look at your products in peace.
- Have a smooth checkout process planned in advance so you aren't fumbling and wasting time.
- Capture email addresses for all new customers. You want to be able to talk with them again.
- Engage and listen to what people have to say about your products. It's a perfect feedback opportunity!

Let's transition now to best practices for communicating with attendees at the show.

Here's the way to "work" a show. I call it the **Exhibitor Interaction Flow.**

Greeting. Say hi! Pretty obvious right? When people walk by your table, greet them even if they are just strolling by and not stopping. Things like "Good morning" or "Love your sweater" or "Thanks for coming out to see us today" will all do.

You are just being friendly and could attract people to stop and chat with you who normally would have passed you up.

One Sentence Explanation. When someone approaches your table and you've greeted them, give a one sentence explanation of what your product is. Make it compelling and include why it stands out. (Your USP from the "Finding the Hidden Treasure" section.)

Your product may not be obvious in terms of what it does. Don't leave them guessing, tell them!

Browse and Consider. Let people look around at their leisure without you hounding them with more and more information. Be available but not hovering. You've already presented a friendly environment that allows them to ask you questions or continue the conversation if they want to.

An Open Invitation Back. If someone leaves without buying anything, close the interaction leaving room for more. It could be a statement like, "Enjoy the show. Thanks for stopping by." Or, "I enjoyed talking with you. Stop back anytime."

You want them to walk away with a good feeling about being in your booth, whether it was for 30 seconds or half an hour.

Who doesn't love parties? Make yours the one everyone wants to attend!

Chapter 42

I DON'T SEE YOU

———————〜———————

A crowd of people huddled around your table at the local craft fair is a blessing. If you know how to manage it that is.

Otherwise it's a curse. People will walk away with a bad taste in their mouth about your business. Even before they tasted your new orange peel cake pops!

Most likely they'll never come back. At worst, they will talk about you and the horrible experience they had.

People don't like to be ignored. We all have an unconscious need to feel valued and significant.

WE ALL HAVE AN UNCONSCIOUS NEED TO FEEL VALUED AND SIGNIFICANT.

But when you're faced with a crowd, how do you keep people involved?

Lana has this mastered. She sells personalized plush animals to the young participants at cheer competitions.

Whether it's a panda bear or a fluffy white puppy, all the stuffed animals are wearing the individual squad's colors. They have a practice hair bow (the uniform bows can only be worn during competition), earrings, a cheer skirt and a custom printed ribbon with the girl's name on one side and her cheer team mascot on the other. You can see why the line at her table is so long.

She does two things at these shows. She brings animals that have been preordered. A good portion of her crowd is there to pay for and pick up their new snuggly treasure.

And she sells. So, the other portion of the crowd wants to place an order. This is more time consuming and adds to the challenge of booth management.

Lana has perfected her systems which is why I want to share her process with you. Whether you have preorders or not, her method of managing a crowd can work for you.

Divide by intent. If, like Lana, you have people coming to see you for different reasons, have two separate places where you can handle the different activities.

Customers picking up pre-ordered products will complete their transaction much quicker. That can be one side of the table.

The other side can be for those placing orders. There you would have sample selections, order forms and whatever else is needed to follow through on a sale.

Remember this is only if your booth gets overcrowded. Otherwise, one person can manage both the tasks; order fulfillment and order taking.

Systematize the ordering process. Most of the time at craft shows the sale transaction is a simple process. Someone picks out what they want to buy, you run their credit card or take their cash, package it up and you're done. If the transaction is any more complicated, having a pre-planned system will make your life so much easier.

Another way to handle this is to have a form that you or your customer fills out. It's complete with all the information you need to process the order. These can be handed out if a line has formed to keep the customer engaged and speed up the process.

The forms are also a fallback if someone can't wait. They can complete the order form on their own and mail it back to you. This isn't ideal, but it could save a sale that may be lost otherwise.

Acknowledge their presence. This can't be overstressed. If you are busy, you obviously can't talk with everyone at once. Plus, you want to stay focused on the individual conversation you are already having.

But you can acknowledge someone who is waiting. Make eye contact, smile and let them know you see them and will be with them shortly. This act of subtle contact starts the engagement process and they are more likely to wait around for their turn.

Have you ever walked in a store or up to a show table and been completely ignored? It doesn't feel good. But if there is even the briefest exchange, most people understand that you're busy and they will wait their turn for a reasonable amount of time.

Offer samples or entertainment. Is there something you can do to provide a distraction while people are waiting in line?

If you have a consumable product, offering samples is a great option.

Lana has her daughter walk up and greet each person waiting. She finds out if they are there to pick up a pre-order or place an order. Then she directs them to the correct line.

She also engages in small talk about what they have or are ordering. What animal and what colors? How did they find out about the plush animals?

Anything to get a customer excited about having their cheer mascot. This is a way for people to stay interested until a transaction can be completed.

Match people up with each other. If you are so busy at your booth you can't possibly interact with everyone, have them start talking with each other!

If you recognize someone in the crowd, let everyone know that she's already a customer and ask,

"What scent candle is your favorite these days?" That may get others talking with her about their intended purchase.

Or, "Margie, let me introduce you to Gina. I believe you two have daughters the same age ..."

All you're trying to do here is make people feel valued, recognized and important. And they are! They are your brand new customers and it's your first "date!"

Chapter 43

IT'S NOT OVER YET

———— ⌒ ————

Oh no! You can't just pack up and call it a day when a show is over.

There are other steps required to make sure each craft show builds upon the others.

It's like a set of blocks. If you put blocks one by one next to each other but separated, you aren't building anything. You only have a lot of individual blocks. But if you stack one on top of another, now you're getting somewhere.

It's the same thing with a trade show or craft fair.

The first thing you'll want to do after a show is fill any orders that were placed. If it wasn't a cash and carry event that is ... or if you took special orders or were out of stock on something.

Timeliness here is important. It's the beginning of a relationship with these customers and you want them to be delighted with the quick turnaround of your order fulfillment.

A nice touch in this case would be to include a special note with the order. Reference them by name and tell them how much you enjoyed meeting them in person. Any extra details of your conversation will impress them and make them feel special too.

With each gesture like this, you are deepening your connection. Also include a flyer highlighting other shows you'll be attending throughout the year.

Next, add them to your mailing list. You did get their email, didn't you?

Gathering emails is the way to stay in touch and make sure future sales are possible. I know you've heard the email topic from me several times throughout this book already. That's because it's so SO important.

Up to this point it's been all about following through on commitments with people who are your new or current customers.

Most likely you've also promised things to others at the show. It may be sending them more information, providing samples or a wholesale price sheet. Turnaround here is important too.

Many show exhibitors are well-intentioned but never follow through on what they say they'll do. Once they are no longer face to face with someone at a show, the promised action is forgotten. It isn't that they don't mean to, it just gets lost in the hectic pace of the event.

Consider having a blank notebook for this purpose. You can write down all these miscellaneous promises. Now take action on these commitments. You will stand out as a true professional and it will be remembered.

Getting back to emails, another project after the show is to log in all the emails you received from people who didn't buy but wanted more information from you.

We talked earlier in the section "I Want to Know You" about tagging your emails.

This group of people can be tagged under Show Prospects. Depending on how fancy you want to get you can even break them out by specific shows. At first, however, I'd keep it simple and just have a general Show Prospect tag.

Finally, you'll want to take stock of the show. How did it perform for you? Consider things like the ease of working the show, the traffic that came through and how close they were to your ideal customer.

Of course, you'll also take into account the sales you made versus the cost participation.

Make notes for yourself so you'll remember what you experienced. This will help you decide if it's a show you should repeat next year. Particularly if you do a lot of events, this will help you remember one versus another.

I'll challenge you each year to drop and add at least one show in your rotation. This allows you to get in front of a new group of people and your shows don't become stale. For you or your customers.

Shows are hard work, but they can be fun at the same time. Each one is different, and you get to meet such interesting people. If you have never experienced one before, I encourage you to do so. This year!

Craft and trade shows are an event in time. There are other aspects of your business that are present every day.

It's easy to get caught up in all the daily tasks that running a business requires. So easy that you forget to step back and see some overarching activities and practices that keep you on track and present possibilities for growth.

For instance, did you know there are actions you can take to actually put yourself in luck's path?

Daily Stuff

---～---

MANICURES
& MASSAGES

I wish I would have had this list of daily truths about running a business when I first started.

It's a combination of advice and concepts that I know to be true. They are hard-earned lessons discovered through experience.

You will learn them too. But it's nice to hear them up front as well.

This first one is something you can take advantage of by being "in the know."

Chapter 44

LUCKY YOU!

———~———

Some people attract good things over and over again. They must be naturally lucky and that's how they've gotten to where they are today.

Is there a little pang of jealousy when you're watching the morning news and up pops Confection Creations? They're a local chocolate shop being highlighted for Valentine's Day. Sure, their dark sea salt truffles are out of this world. You're happy for them. But how did they get this opportunity? Why couldn't that have been you?

Then there's Shellie whose luxurious coconut oil body lotion is now on the shelves at Whole Foods.

You work just as hard and your product is just as good but you're not in Whole Foods.

You think, *They are just so lucky.*

Or are they?

Here's the problem with luck. It's a lie and a cop out. It's an excuse you can conveniently use to explain why you are not progressing and seeing the success that others are.

Would you like to start getting lucky too? It's not as random or mysterious as it might seem.

The trick to being lucky is to put yourself in luck's path.

THE TRICK TO BEING LUCKY IS TO PUT YOURSELF IN LUCK'S PATH.

Luck will not find you if you stay in your home office and hide behind a computer screen hanging out on Facebook. You need to take chances. Be open and observant for opportunities and take action when they cross your path.

You're out to lunch with a friend and you find out she knows someone in the divisional office of a chain store you'd like to be in. Ask her if she'll make an introduction.

You are part of a Facebook group and there is a discussion on the success you can have at craft shows. Engage in that discussion. Ask questions. Connect with others through direct messages. Or take other actions that can help advance you toward your goal.

The next time you're at the coffee shop be aware of the conversations around you. Engage in small talk with the people in line with you. It can be at the most random moment when an opportunity presents itself.

Chat with the person next to you on the airplane. Take interest when you meet someone new at a dinner party.

While doing final edits for this book, I took a break and went into a new store, Vintage Bliss & Co., in my neighborhood. Wouldn't you know, the owner, Nancy is a designer and has two co-op locations displaying products from local artists.

After further discussion, I have now scheduled my first book signing at Queen Bee Artisan Market in Lake Geneva, WI. Not bad use of a 30-minute lunch break!

Everyday life events are a breeding ground for spontaneous lucky moments. Watch for them.

It's in this way that you can take control of your own luck barometer and increase your chances of being the one others refer to as lucky.

Chapter 45

WHAT'S AROUND THAT CORNER?

———————— ∽ ————————

I wish someone would have told me this when I first started. I was so naive. You may be too.

I honestly believed I could create a business that would have none of the problems that I'd heard about from others.

My website would be enticing and load quickly. I would treat my customers so well that word of mouth would bring in all the sales I needed. My systems from inquiry follow-up to product fulfillment would be world class. In summary, my business would be the model for others to emulate.

Why did I think this? Because I was the one creating it. I knew my intentions were solid and I was determined.

But I was living in a fantasy land.

I didn't take into account that there would be times when vendors would take days to fill an order. I didn't think about deliveries being delayed due to severe weather. I didn't consider internet outages or unreasonable customers lashing out at employees. Or the myriad of issues that arise.

What I wish someone would have told me is that being a business owner means you need to become an efficient problem solver.

Okay, I'm a quick learner. I get it, problems will arise that I'll need to deal with.

But I was in for another realization.

At that point I thought I could easily manage these problems from time to time. Even though I'm a perfectionist, I could handle the imperfect and find the adjustments that needed to be made to get back on track.

I grew frustrated though. Why was it that I'd no sooner resolve one problem than another would appear? I'd work through that one and then two more would need my attention. Seriously, what was I doing wrong?

Finally, and I mean finally, I came to understand that there will always be an open list of issues requiring my attention. That's part of being the owner.

What I now know and what I want to reinforce to you is this. It's inevitable that there will always be problems on your plate. It's part of what you bought into. It's a reality you just have to accept.

Consider yourself told!

Chapter 46

HUMPTY DUMPTY

―――――~―――――

Have you heard the concept of working "in your business" versus working "on your business?"

Changing that one little letter and understanding what it means can have a profound effect on your ability to grow your company.

Let's get some definitions going here.

Working "IN" your business.

This is where you are when you start. You have no choice but to work *in* your business because you are doing literally everything. From determining what vendors to use, to paperwork, marketing and promotion. Then there's making the product (if applicable), filling and shipping orders, it's all on you, baby!

Working "ON" your business.

This is the high level visionary stuff. It's strategy, projections and planning. It starts with your initial dream of what you want to create. Then it continues as you set plans in motion to reach that dream. Along the way new opportunities or an enhanced vision may be identified that you want to pursue.

This happened with Karyn at Little Pink Ladybug. Her business started with making little girl hair bows and selling them to local boutiques.

A few years later, while working *on* her business, she identified a new opportunity.

Her company now offers hairbow templates. This way others can create the beautiful intricate bows that Karyn designs.

Recently, she had another vision, a tool that could cut ribbon in a V shape and heat seal the edges at the same time. That's how the BowVy came into existence.

The evolution of Little Pink Ladybug happened when Karyn was working *on* her business and advancing it toward the next phase.

I hope this example gives you a clear picture and helps you understand the difference between working *on* versus working *in* your business.

It's a continual struggle to not repeatedly be drawn back into working *in* your business. It's as if there is a magnet trying to attract you back in at every turn.

It's imperative that you resist this pull.

Getting stuck working only *in* the business leads to a stall in sales.

GETTING STUCK WORKING ONLY *IN* THE BUSINESS LEADS TO A STALL IN SALES.

You will have to do a combination of both. But recognizing which one you are doing at any given time is important.

Then it is critical that you dedicate enough time to work *on* your business so you can grow.

Chapter 47

NOW I KNOW

What is the number one thing that prevents someone from starting a business?

It's one little four-letter word: F.E.A.R.

Fear stops us in our tracks. Even our best intentions get sidetracked with excuses. Supporting those excuses, when it comes down to it, is that we get scared.

It helps to acknowledge that everyone ... even the most successful among us ... gets scared at times. Human nature has provided us with enough self-doubt to last a lifetime.

We ask ourselves if we really know what we're talking about.

We decide that our designs aren't anything special and a competitor's are so much better.

We psyche ourselves out because there is another handmade candy shop in the neighboring town. Why should we open another?

We wonder if we'll be found out because maybe we're really a fraud.

Have you ever been told that your input helped someone out? Or that your product is beautiful?

Customers drive miles and miles to Adrian's Boutique in Buhler, KS because they love the atmosphere and product selection. For some, it's a weekend event to visit Vicki's shop.

If any version of this has happened to you even once, then you are not a fraud.

Since we've already established that this will never go away, you need to remind yourself that you are putting good out into the world. It's worth talking back to your petty little fear companion who pops up all the time.

"The cave you fear to enter holds the treasure you seek." ~James Campbell

You have to get comfortable with being uncomfortable. To enter the cave that holds your treasure. Your dream and your profitable business await you on the other side.

Chapter 48

98.6

———⌇———

Scott was a criminal defense attorney in Wisconsin ... until the day he had a heart attack in the courthouse. He survived but closed his briefcase on his 18-year career and went off in search of a less stressful life.

Today he's the happiest he's ever been as the founder of Twice Baked Pottery. Scott's life is full and busy being a potter and exhibiting at over 40 shows a year. He's healthy and full of life.

For Scott, being a business owner has its ups and downs, but he checks his health and stays in tune with his stress levels. He's one of the lucky ones.

I don't think most people who start up a business truly understand how stressful it can be. They choose this life as an entrepreneur because it seems to be full of freedom and spare time. Talk to anyone who has experience and they'll tell you that's the furthest from the truth.

Having your own business is full of rewards but it's hard work and dedication that gets results. That means time in. Successes and failures. Sleepless nights. AND satisfaction and money.

HAVING YOUR OWN BUSINESS IS FULL OF REWARDS BUT IT'S HARD WORK AND DEDICATION THAT GETS RESULTS.

It's so easy to sacrifice for the company.

I've done it myself. I'll think, *There's no time to get to the dentist or have that regular checkup. I'll get to it in a few months.*

Then a year goes by and somewhere along the line health appointments get dropped from the "to do" list.

Work life balance may sound like a mellow topic. But continual daily stress and compounding responsibilities can lead to serious health issues. It can wipe away all that you've worked so hard to create. Or worse.

It is imperative that you stay aware and up to date on everything that relates to your well-being. If you don't, all you've worked so hard to build will be for nothing.

Chapter 49

OOPS!

———～———

After over 150 episodes of my podcast there is one thing I've heard in different versions over and over again.

Someone has an idea and starts a business based on this idea. Then over time it morphs into a new version of the original idea. Or something else entirely forms as an extension of the first idea.

It's in the adjustments to the original plan where unique products and businesses rise to the top.

IT'S IN THE ADJUSTMENTS TO THE ORIGINAL PLAN WHERE UNIQUE PRODUCTS AND BUSINESSES RISE TO THE TOP.

Sometimes these things happen by accident as with Tim of Burton's Maplewood Farm. As the name suggests, he produces barrel aged maple syrup.

Tim never could have imagined how one of their now famous techniques would be discovered.

One day while doing some housekeeping in the maple house, Tim decided to move what he thought was an empty cask. It was next to the huge Rumford fireplace.

Much to his surprise, the barrel contained about 30 gallons of syrup. It had been sitting near the fireplace for well over a year.

Tim tasted the syrup and was met with a deep flavor unlike any of the other syrup flavors they had ever made.

He was quick to understand why. This cask was previous used to age Apple Jack Brandy. The heat from the fireplace had created an entirely new depth of flavor to his maple syrup!

That forgotten cask was the genesis of a method now coined "Fire Infusion."

All from a forgotten cask left in a forgotten place that over time performed its magic.

Sheila of Brownie Brittle had a similar single moment of enlightenment.

Her whole life she loved the corner pieces of brownies. You know, the crunchy edges that are on both sides of a corner and are crisper than the rest.

In her brownie business Sheila had a routine. In the afternoons she would go into the production area and take some corner pieces as a snack.

One day she got there early and saw that her line people were doing the same thing.

It was at that moment she identified that she wasn't the only one who loved the corners, and the crunchy side drippings for that matter.

Sheila speculated that there could be a world of people out there who would be fans if she created a version of these crispy brownies. And there are!

These stories go to show you, be aware—when something looks like scrap or turns out wrong—it may be just right!

Chapter 50

IT'S A TEST

———————◡———————

Taking initiative and always learning is the sign of a progressive small business owner.

One way to do this is through taking an online course. Many of us (myself included) have gone through courses but afterwards go back to our old routines and move through the days as we always have.

Status quo.

Doing this is a waste of your investment—both in time and money.

Here are the seven steps you should follow that will allow any course you take to provide the most value it possibly can.

Set Up. Upon registration you will receive a few emails. Look for an invoice and your personal login credentials that include the website, your username and your password. Set up a system to capture this information so you can find it easily. It may be a file on your computer. Or it could be a folder within your email.

I use g-mail so that I can always access my courses regardless of which computer I'm using (or phone or iPad).

I have a master folder called Training Programs. Underneath I have sub-folders labeled with each course. When I'm done or no longer access the course on a regular basis, I hide the labels. The folder is still there and accessible but hiding it keeps my email sidebar cleaner. So only my active courses are visible.

Define Your Objective. Once you're all set up, write down on paper the result you expect from taking the course.

This will keep you focused and attentive. That way you can capture information specific to your goal.

If you're keeping a notebook write the word "Objective" as the very first note. Then jot down your intentions—what you want to be able to do differently or better as a result of taking the course.

Schedule Class Time. You want to be fully present when you take your course. That means no distractions. No email, no phone calls, no Facebook. Be focused so you don't miss any of the nuances or specific comments that could be the golden nugget you were needing.

By doing this you'll go through the course faster and you'll capture all the valuable information. You'll be in a learning zone. This will allow you to uncover ideas and applications that might be missed if you're distracted.

Start at the Beginning. Resist the urge to jump ahead and start in the middle of a program. You may feel you're well beyond some of the introductory topics in a course. But if you start in the middle, you don't know what one sentence or single point in the beginning is a treasure that will remain buried forever because you didn't uncover it.

If you stay present and aren't distracted, you can quickly get through the initial portions. Then you'll be ready to move on to new concepts knowing all your bases are covered.

Continue through the course in order. Most programs are built to be sequential. One module builds upon another. You may lose time having to go back to find or learn something you didn't know you needed.

Participate in All Add-Ons. If your course includes a private Facebook Group or another opportunity to connect with others taking the course, by all means join in.

Some of the best lessons learned are in these groups. Discussions come up on topics you may not have thought about. The responses and subsequent conversations can be extremely helpful.

Plus, this is an opportunity to meet people. These new relationships might become the most valuable part of taking the course.

Create an Implementation Plan. You've learned a lot. NOW, how are you going to apply what you've learned to advance your business? What are you going to implement or do differently?

This is where many people fail. Yes, a big "F" in the course!

You need to act upon what you've just learned!

Create an action plan to implement what you now know.

If your goal is to create a change in the way you do things, remember it takes time for change to become a routine. That means you have to consciously integrate it into your daily activities.

In your plan, write down exactly what you'll do differently. Make it specific and attainable.

You may want to create a list of things you'd like to affect. Then select one. Get that going until it's second nature and then move on to next one.

By following these seven steps, you can have confidence that your course investments will produce positive outcomes.

Chapter 51

YOUR "GO TO" PEOPLE

———~———

Masterminds are very popular these days. They are helpful no matter where you are in your business journey.

Napoleon Hill introduced this concept back in the 1930's in his book, *Think and Grow Rich*. He defines a mastermind group as, "The coordination of knowledge and effort of two or more people, who work toward a definite purpose, in the spirit of harmony."

To put it in simpler terms, today masterminds are organized groups of business owners who meet on a regular basis to help each other grow their respective businesses.

There are both free and paid masterminds and the results, when you have a strong group, can be astounding.

I was part of a mastermind group that existed for over 10 years. We disbanded about four months ago. It wasn't because it was no longer valuable. It was because several of our members had either sold their business or by choice moved on to a different focus in life. We called ourselves Girls in Business (GIBs).

Last Monday I returned home from six weeks of travel. It was a combination of three business trips and one vacation all bumped up against one another. You can imagine when I got to the office how much there was to do.

An emergency message came through on my phone that Linda, one of my GIBs, desperately needed to talk. Could we possibly have an emergency meeting? Soon? In an hour?

Well of course! All things stop for my GIBs. We assembled and worked through a serious and timely issue that needed to be addressed. Of course, Linda could have moved forward on her own. She's an established and successful leader of her company. But on this one, she felt she needed to call in the forces to confirm her course of action.

This illustrates the benefit of a mastermind group. No groundwork needed to be laid to get to the topic. We knew each other's businesses as if they were our own. We had been together so long that there was a strong bond of trust and faith in the good-intentions of all members.

We immediately got to the point and gave our input. Linda left with renewed confidence and a plan she instituted right away.

Being a mastermind member so important to me that I've already joined a more structured group. It's a high-level and high-priced commitment. My group is made up of women business owners from all over the country. We meet every other week on the phone and three times a year in person. It is a group run by an experienced leader who specializes in masterminds.

You can join a structured paid mastermind like this. Or you can start your own mastermind group right in your local community.

Here are some best practices for putting together your own group.

1. The optimal group size is 6-8 members.
2. Set up a meeting schedule that will work for everyone. Meeting every two weeks for 1 1/2 - 2 hours at a time is optimal. The meetings can be conducted in person or online through a tool like Zoom.
3. Each member must commit to the importance of showing up to each meeting. Your meetings need to be a priority and not cancelled or rescheduled at random. When one member doesn't take part, they are out of the loop. If absences occur too often, the group will fall apart because you can't make progress. You have to repeat information to get an absent member up to speed. It also shows disrespect to the group and the bond will deteriorate.
4. When picking members, all participants should be at approximately the same stage in their business development. That way everyone is learning and advancing and all members can give suggestions and receive advice.
5. Here's the basic flow of a meeting: You start by reviewing focus topics that each member committed to from the prior

meeting. (Obviously, you won't have this for the very first meeting.)

Then each member has time on the "hot seat" where they bring up an issue they are encountering. The more detailed the topic the better. A timer is set (20-30 minutes each) and you all work together to help come to a solution or direction for the given topic.

If you have a large group of eight members, four people can be on the hot seat each meeting. After the hot seats, you each go around and share with the group what your focus is for the next two weeks. This is what you're accountable to report back on at the beginning of the following meeting.

6. Someone should document what happens at the meeting and capture the focus goal each person commits to for the upcoming two weeks. This can be done by one designated person or the responsibility can be passed around the group.

Masterminds. Definitely something to consider.

I've just explained how to overcome fear, accept problems and look for the opportunity in accidents.

We've also talked about options for personal business growth through taking courses and joining masterminds.

As your business journey progresses, there may come a time when your business is not the right fit for you anymore.

This does not need to be a downer. Wait until you hear what Julie did!

Closing Shop

---~---

NIGHTY NIGHT

Every business goes through a lifecycle.

Based on the product offering it could span two years or decades.

What if your business today was making wagon wheels? No market.

What about cassettes for tape recorders? No market. (Some of you may need to google this!)

How about Polly Pockets or Skip-Its or Crazy Bones ... all things that don't hold interest for today's audience. They've run through their lifecycle.

You *can* have control over this lifecycle when it comes to your business.

Ben and Blake are a perfect example. They are third generation owners of The Village Common. The way each generation stayed in existence was by adjusting their product to meet the needs of the market. By doing so they remained relevant as interests and the culture changed.

Let's finish up here with a talk about lifecycle and your options.

Chapter 52

CHANGE YOUR WAYS

———————— ∼ ————————

With every business and every product, there is a natural life cycle. It consists of five stages. Let's talk about this in relation to your company.

Planning. This is the time when, behind the scenes, you are setting everything in place to start your business. You file the legal registrations and do things to set up shop. These include building a website, buying inventory, etc. It's a time when you are putting a lot of money into development.

Start Up. What you've been waiting for! Your Grand Opening and the introduction of your business to the market starts here. During this time there are low sales and high costs. In this stage the company starts to gain traction and attract attention.

Growth. Once you're open and promoting the business, sales grow and there comes a point where sales surpass costs. In other words, you begin to make money.

Maturity. This is the time when you've hit your stride. You are known to be the one to go to for whatever it is you sell. Because of your reputation, sales come in easily and your profits are strong. You want to stay here as long as you can.

Decline. Demand for what you offer goes down, as do sales. The excitement that was once there for your product or service is harder to attract. It becomes a struggle to make ends meet. Eventually the company has run its course and closes.

Ugh. This Decline stage sounds terrible.

But what happens with regard to this business life cycle is up to you. It starts with understanding that this progression is normal.

When you're aware of the business life cycle, you can be on the lookout as you advance through these stages.

With a product, this progression is inevitable, although the advancement may take years or even decades to reach Decline.

Think of products that were the "in" thing and faded over time. There are millions! Boom Boxes, Pac-Man and Teenage Mutant Ninja Turtles.

In fashion you can see it change quickly. Straight legs change to bell bottoms. Shoulder pads turn to shoulder cutouts. Lace, denim, floral patterns ... they've all had their time in the limelight. Then they all turned to being yesterday's style.

If your business revolves around one product, you need to be very attentive so you can identify when the tide starts to turn.

Check periodically to ensure your product is still relevant with regard to the trends taking place around you.

If, or should I say *when,* your product starts to lose relevancy, you have two options.

You can cut your losses and close shop.

Or you can reposition yourself in a way where what you sell stays up with the times.

That could be by tweaking your product to make it new again. Or to switch your offerings entirely to be fresh and up to date. Then customers still see your company as on point with the times.

Being blind to this concept has caught even the biggest companies unaware. Where once video rental stores were in almost every neighborhood, they are non-existent today. The same thing sadly is happening with book stores right now.

Times change, and you need to stay in step to stay in business.

Chapter 53

MOVING NEXT DOOR

———∼———

Sometimes the best option for an underperforming business is to cut the financial and emotional cord and shut down.

To carry on because you want to see it through to success no matter what is pointless and can lead to disaster.

There is no harm or shame in closing shop. Mark your learning off to gained experience that you can use if you decide to enter into a new venture.

There is another option to consider however, if your problem is declining sales and covering your costs.

Julie discovered this in the nick of time.

Out of college Julie worked at and eventually purchased The Silk Thumb, a silk floral shop she'd been with all through high school.

This is where she discovered her love for flowers and found that she has a sense of style and design skill too. It was only natural for her to come back and work in the same shop where her passion began.

Call it fortuitous or a calculated plan. When the owner of the shop was ready to sell, there Julie was as the obvious one to pick up and continue the business.

It was a good decision too. The store had a stellar reputation and the perfect retail location. Julie knew all the systems to run the business, so the transition was effortless as well.

As will happen, times changed and the depression of the late 90's hit. Julie saw her sales go down and down. Silk floral arrangements were a luxury expense after all. Even in this upscale community, her product was in less demand by no fault of her own.

I visited Julie in her shop one day and as we talked I saw her eyes grow blurry. The single tear that started down her cheek led to a flood when I asked if she was okay.

Along with the tears came an explanation of her deep sadness in the realization that she would need to close her doors. She felt responsible for the fate of the business. It hit particularly hard because she felt she had let down the first owner.

It was heartbreaking. All the work that went into buying and running her business and then having to close the door for the last time was gut-wrenching.

I couldn't get her off my mind. But I could help ease the financial loss by participating in her closeout sales.

A couple of weeks later I was going to pick up my order and I was met with a completely different Julie. She was upbeat, smiling and full of energy.

Wait ... what did I miss?

Julie had taken the fate of The Silk Thumb into her own hands. Yes, she had to close down the retail shop. But she was turning retail in for something greater. She devised a plan of transformation for the business that would fit the current market situation.

Today, The Silk Thumb exists as a silk floral design center. It's housed in a studio accessible by appointment only. Her designs are placed in high rise apartments and prominent lobbies in downtown Chicago. Even in prestigious waiting rooms, lounges and CEO offices.

Not only that, Julie is now married and a new mom. She has time to spend with her family in ways that never would have been possible when she had a brick and mortar shop.

Now Julie's reputation and her bank account continue to grow.

This could have been a story of defeat. But today Julie can stand proud as she presents a story of rejuvenation and success.

Yes, there is a time when it's right to close the doors. But before you do, think of Julie's story and see if a version of it could hold true for you.

CONCLUSION

We have now been through over 50 best practices. Follow them to ensure that your dream of turning your hobby or craft into a business can actually come true.

In writing this book, I've had you on my mind the entire time. I feel like we know each other and I'm excited for you to continue on a journey like no other.

If you take these points to heart and act accordingly, wonderful things are going to happen in your life.

Your business will thrive. You will have the pride of creating a company that is a part of and represents you.

This excites me because it means your art will be shared with the world.

I'd like to keep the conversation going and welcome any comments you have for me.

I'd like to know about your dream. Or tell me what you think of the book and thoughts on any of the points here. You can reach me through email at sue@suemonhait.com

In the Resources section you'll find the tools I mentioned throughout the book that can provide further guidance.

I'd also be honored to have you as part of my free but private Facebook Group called Gift Biz Breeze.

There you will find a community of like-minded and supportive creators. They are traveling through their own creative business journeys just like you.

Finally, keep in mind another free resource which is the Gift Biz Unwrapped podcast. You can find it in on Apple Podcasts (iTunes), Stitcher, YouTube and on our website at Gift Biz Unwrapped.com

It's time for you to take action, go show the world what you've got.

I'm cheering you on!

REFERENCES

Included in this book are references to businesses both real and fictitious.

Sometimes the identity has been masked based on the topic being discussed.

Since many of these businesses are ones I believe you are looking to aspire to, I want to highlight them.

They are examples of what can result when you dream big, take action, experiment and fail, and rise up to try again.

Take a look at their websites and hear their stories from my podcast. If it's in your heart, support these companies with purchases or even a shout

out that you saw their inclusion here and wish them well.

I look forward to the day when you too can be listed on a page like this. Maybe even on one of mine!

Adrian's Boutique –
giftbizunwrapped.com/vickiadrian

Alden's Kennels
giftbizunwrapped.com/aldenskennels

Bluegrass –
giftbizunwrapped.com/bluegrass

Burton's Maplewood Farm -
giftbizunwrapped.com/burtonsmaplewoodfarm

Brownie Brittle –
giftbizunwrapped.com/browniebrittle

Cedar and Rush –
giftbizunwrapped.com/cedarandrush

Celebrate Sweetly –
giftbizunwrapped.com/celebratesweetly

Gaspara Flora –
giftbizunwrapped.com/gasparaflora

Home and Company –
giftbizunwrapped.com/homeandcompany

Kara's Vineyard Wedding –
giftbizunwrapped.com/karasvineyardwedding

Kuhfs –
giftbizunwrapped.com/kuhfs

Little Pink Ladybug –
giftbizunwrapped.com/littlepinkladybug

Lucas Candies –
giftbizunwrapped.com/lucascandies

Lula's Bath and Bombs -
giftbizunwrapped.com/lulasbathandbombs

Make A Memory -
giftbizunwrapped.com/lanahorton

Marshmallow MBA –
giftbizunwrapped.com/marshmallowmba

Maureen's Sweet Shoppe –
giftbizunwrapped.com/maureenssweetshoppe

My Secret Garden –
giftbizunwrapped.com/mysecretgarden

Pinzit –
giftbizunwrapped.com/pinzit

Queen Bee Artisan Market –
giftbizunwrapped.com/queenbeeartisanmarket

Santa Barbara Gift Baskets –
giftbizunwrapped.com/annepazier

Shopping for a Change –
giftbizunwrapped.com/staceyhorowitz

Squirrel Away Bird Café –
giftbizunwrapped.com/squirrelaway

The Leakey Collection –
giftbizunwrapped.com/katyleakey

The Mad Soyentist –
giftbizunwrapped.com/madsoyentist

The Ribbon Print Company –
theribbonprintcompany.com

The Silk Thumb –
giftbizunwrapped.com/juliebrugioni

The Village Common –
giftbizunwrapped.com/villagecommon

Tuscany Tours –
giftbizunwrapped.com/tuscanytours

Twice Baked Pottery –
giftbizunwrapped.com/twicebakedpottery

RESOURCES FROM GIFT BIZ UNWRAPPED

FREE LEARNING AND SUPPORT

Gift Biz Breeze Facebook Group is a community of creators just like you who come together to share ideas, resources, and tips as you follow your entrepreneurial path. Search for the group on Facebook and request to join. We can't wait to welcome you in!

Gift Biz Unwrapped Podcast is a weekly show offering insights and advice to develop and grow your business. Catch the show on Apple Podcasts (iTunes), Stitcher, YouTube and on our website at giftbizunwrapped.com

TOOLS

Name Generator Workbook takes you through an exercise to come up with a unique name for your business or a new product so that it stands out and represents you.

giftbizunwrapped.com/namegenerator

Network Ninja Course offers guidance on how to get the most out of your networking efforts. Networking is your fast track to getting business. But many people stay away because it's scary. What if you enter a room and don't know a single soul? What should you say when you have to stand up and do an elevator speech in front of a room full of people? It's not hard when you know exactly what to do.

giftbizunwrapped.com/networkninja

As a thank you for reading my book, I'm offering this $50 course to you for free. To accept your gift, email sue@suemonhait.com and type "Free Networking Course" in the subject line.

MAKERS MBA

If you're looking for a detailed step by step program to get your business up and running. This is the program to check out. It ensures that you start your company on a solid foundation so it's poised to be profitable and thrive. For more details go to giftbizunwrapped.com/makersmba.

ACKNOWLEDGEMENTS

———～———

I've had this book not just in my head but outlined and ready to write for the last two years. What stopped me? Nothing. I only needed to put it first on the priority list. Finally, its time has come.

Maker to Master represents another chapter in my entrepreneurial journey and another way to support an artisan community that I adore. You know I call you the Gifters-Bakers-Crafters-Makers ... all of you who have talents that many envy.

It is my honor to share what I know about starting and growing a business, so you can get your art out into the world. We all want it. It makes our life richer and our spirits sing.

"You are the average of the five people you spend the most time with."

This quote by Jim Rohn couldn't be more true. I am blessed that the people around me are supportive in everything I do. Perhaps I've unconsciously structured it that way.

It starts with my parents, Mary Jane and Robert Wheatley who had praise and love for me at every turn. I know I was fortunate to have their support and they provided a solid base off of which I could jump and take risks.

When I met the man of my dreams; my dear husband, Michael, I knew my life could continue in the same way. He has always provided a safety net of love and guidance as I learned the challenges of being a woman in the corporate environment of the late 80s and 90s. I thrived under his support and captured much of the experience I use today because I could endure and flourish in those times.

Sales results don't lie regardless of your gender. Michael taught me how to have tough skin and go outside my comfort zone long before this was a theme. I love you for that and so much more, "Mikey."

To my children, David and Nichole who are my reason for living. You have taught me more than you know. I'm not talking about the mispronouncing of almost every word that you so often tease me about. I'm talking about being true to yourself. Being ambitious and stretching for almost out of reach dreams. I'm talking about the blessing of watching you both grow into adults with so much to offer the world—in your own ways—with your own style.

Friendships. Right beside family are my dear friends. Here's a bird's eye view:

High School Friends - Who knew we'd still be so close even now? Patti, Robin, Debbie, Shelia, Erin, Beth, Deb, Barb, Pam, Stacey, Meg, Barbara and our late Connie. When we're together nothing changes. I can go back in time and instantly experience the carefree days of our youth. We are so blessed to have each other. I smile when I think of us.

Friday Night Girls - It's the beacon at the end of my week. Knowing we'll be together is like an oasis in this crazy business life of mine. Debbie, Gwenda, Barb, Lauri, Caryn and Nancy even though you're far away now. Cheers!

Girls in Business - My first mastermind group even though we didn't know that's what it was called. Linda and Robyn, the three of us are the last ones standing. I know I can reach out to you anytime I need advice. I'm so proud of both of you.

A few specific public shoutouts here.

Patti Gianaras - Thank you for always telling me the truth even when it's tough to hear.

Debbie Masaracchia - Thank you for being supportive right from the start. Remember our Starbucks coffee dates with all my crazy business ideas? I think I narrowed in on the right ones. Don't you?

Gwenda Burkhardt - For your unwavering emotional support. You've always made me feel I can do no wrong. Even though it's not true, I need to hear this sometimes!

Claudia Johnson - My dear SMS. Your faith and contagious positive energy make the world a better place. I cherish hummingbird pictures from your backyard. It reminds me that I love nature and need to balance my work with real life.

Team Gift Biz and Ribbon Print - Lauri, Barb, Anita, Mich, and Renee. You are all the best there is at what you do. Lauri, you are a big catalyst to getting this book published. I'll never forget your response when I told you I finally decided to hire a coach. I was anxious about the investment but knew it was the only way to get this moving forward. I messaged you about what I just did. Your response ... "It's about time. You've been talking about doing this for years!" That's all I needed to hear to be okay about my investment. Thank you.

This single action led to my connection with Lise Cartwright, my publishing coach from Self Publishing School. This book would still be in outline form if not for you. Thank you for guiding me to bring this book to life. I love having a new friend in Perth too!

To my editorial team over at Happy Self Publishing, Sushmita Naroor and Qat Wanders: you have added professionalism and style to my manuscript and final book. A heartfelt thank you.

The wonderful thing about an entrepreneur's journey is that connections continue to be made. I look forward to deepening relationships with my

Biz Chix CEO Mastermind group, my new hire, Sofia, and I am excited to see who else enters into my life in the future.

To all who read this, now is your time to take action. Please take the chance to bring your dream into full focus and make it a reality.

What if dreams actually can come true?

ABOUT THE AUTHOR

Sue Monhait is the founder and CEO of Gift Biz Unwrapped and The Ribbon Print Company.

Besides being an entrepreneur, she's a podcaster and speaker.

Sue worked in the corporate world for almost 20 years consulting over a hundred small, medium and large businesses in market positioning, advertising and sales. She had no idea that all her accumulated knowledge would provide such a solid path for her future.

She has been identified as an industry trendsetter and now focuses on the Gifting-Baking-Crafting-Making spaces. Pulling from her vast experience,

Sue guides people who have a hobby or creative passion that they want to turn into a business. As an extension, she works with existing business owners who have gotten stuck and are looking for that one thing that's needed for them to gain traction and move ahead.

Born and raised in the northern Chicago suburbs, Sue has remained in the area and currently lives in Highland Park, IL with her husband of 32 years, Michael, and their two dogs, Tiger and Panther (not intentionally named after cats!)

As an empty-nester, she watches and supports from afar as her children, David and Nichole, experiment with different areas of the country to call home in their quest to fulfill their own dreams. The entrepreneurial torch has definitely been passed on.

For more, go to giftbizunwrapped.com/meet-sue

.